The 63 Year Old Probie

VICTOR HOFFER

The 63 Year Old Probie
Copyright © 2019 by Victor Hoffer

ISBN: 978-1-7328924-3-9 (Paperback)
ISBN: 978-1-7328924-4-6 (Ebook)

Book Designer: Sarah Katreen Hoggatt

10 9 8 7 6 5 4 3 2 1

Printed and bound in the United States of America
Third edition: January 2, 2019

Bible verses taken from various translations
or translated by the author.

Contents

Acronyms

ADA	Americans with Disablities Act
BASICS	British Association of Immediate Care, Ipswich, England
BC	Battalion Chief
BVM	Bag Valve Mask, used to breathe for a person
CBG	Capillary Blood Glucose
Code 3	When red lights and sirens are being used
COPD	Chronic Obstructive Pulmonary Disease
CPAP	Continuous Positive Airway Pressure, used to help a person breathe
DC	Deputy Chief
DPSST	Department of Public Safety Standards and Training
DUII	Driving Under the Influence of Intoxicants
EDITH	Exit Drills in the Home
edX Class	edX is an online school offering many free courses
EKG	Electrocardiogram is a recording of the heart abbreviated ECG and EKG
EMS	Emergency Medical Services
EMT	Emergency Medical Technician
FDNY	Fire Department of New York
FTEP	Field Training and Evaluation Program
GAC	Governor's Advisory Committee
ICU	Intensive Care Unit
IM	Intramuscular, an injection into the muscle

IO	Intraosseous line, the process of injecting directly into the marrow of the bone
IV	Intravenous line, the process of injecting directly into a vein
LPM	Liters per minute, generally a measurement for oxygen administration
MCFD	Marion County Fire District #1
MCFD#1	Marion County Fire District #1
MDA	Muscular Dystrophy Association
MVC	Motor Vehicle Crash
NHTSA	National Highway Traffic Safety Administration
non-STEMI	Not a ST-Elevation Myocardial Infarction, a heart attack without elevation on the EKG
NREMT	National Registry of Emergency Medical Technicians
O2	Oxygen
OCC	Oregon Convention Center
ODOT	Oregon Department of Transportation
OHA	Oregon Health Authority
OHSU	Oregon Health & Science University
OTC	Oregon Transportation Commission
OTSC	Oregon Transportation Safety Committee
PFC	Patient Flow Coordinator
RN	Registered Nurse
SHED	Salem Hospital Emergency Department
STEMI	ST-Elevation Myocardial Infarction, a heart attack with elevation on the EKG
TEDx	TEDx is a talk that showcases speakers in an under 18 minute presentation (Technology, Entertainmant and Design)
TOD	Tour of Duty, a volunteer who covers a 24 hour shift at the fire station
TSAP	Transportation Safety Action Plan
UCLA	University of California – Los Angeles

USCG	United States Coast Guard
US-DOT	United States Department of Transportation
UTL	Unable to locate
VA	Veterans Administration
VF	Ventricular fibrillation, a life-threatening heart rhythm, results in death

INTRODUCTION

THE 63 YEAR OLD PROBIE is about my year as a newly-hired paramedic with Marion County Fire District #1 in Salem, Oregon. Now that my year is complete, I feel better than I did a year ago. Over those twelve months, I was able to accomplish something that not everyone is able to do, at any age.

My reputation is one of a resilient person and I *am* resilient. I have been through many heartbreaking events—events that were heartbreaking for me and often heartbreaking for my patients and their families. I am strong and have, up to now, stayed away from allowing anyone to see or hear my frailties.

This is why I have hesitated to share this book with anyone. My persona is one of strength and thick skin with hardened steel armor, which, of course, creates its own heavy burden. I have worked hard at not allowing anyone to know that cruel death affects me just like everyone else.

You will hear about my dad and my son who are dead. I miss them with an unending ache and wish they were still alive to give me their love, share my stories, and help me carry my burdens. You will learn of the many things that must be completed on a daily basis at a fire station and the many extra chores a person has to complete as a probationary employee and a paramedic on an ambulance.

Finally, you will feel my disappointments with myself, find out how I work through them, and where I find my strength. You will see me when I am sad and will rejoice with me in small victories. I am going to take my chances with letting you see me just as I am.

Even with the disappointments, this thing I do, taking care of people on an ambulance, is the only real job for me. It is what I do best.

My wish is that you will find faith and hope, strength and resilience, and give love and charity to one another, to *all* people, without regard for recognition or reward.

September

I AM A NEW RECRUIT. AT 63 years old, I never thought I would be going on such an adventure this close to retirement but life leads us into unexpected places when we've made other plans. Thus, I found myself at the Paramedic Academy at the local fire district station training with four other men far younger than myself to be "single role paramedics," eager to serve the public and prove myself during my first year of probation.

Though the new position is an adventure in itself, I am not new to the field. Many years ago, I wrote the first EMT/paramedic Field Training and Evaluation Program (FTEP) book for the state. I have worked over 36 years in the field and have trained hundreds of new paramedics. Then, for the last six months, I've worked for the district on an ambulance as a temporary employee and have now earned a permanent position. Though the last six months doesn't count toward my probation, I won't have to repeat their training program.

FIRE ACADEMY

AT THE FIRE DISTRICT'S LOCAL PARAMEDIC academy, there are five of us who have been hired to be paramedics. We five are called "single role paramedics" as there are two paramedics in an ambulance and the other is both a firefighter *and* paramedic. A firefighter-paramedic and a paramedic run an ambulance, often simply called a medic. The academy runs all week long and we spend the time reviewing the district's policies and procedures, learning how to use the computer charting program, and reviewing protocols on how to treat our patients. Out of the other four new recruits, I have previously trained one, supervised two, and oversaw the volunteer work of the fourth during my time as a temp.

One day, while we were at the academy, one of the other recruits asked me when it was that I got my paramedic license and I told them I got my NREMT Paramedic license in 1982. It suddenly became very quiet as they realized that none of them had been born yet! The next oldest to me was 33 years my junior and the youngest was nine years younger still.

And so it has come to be that with 36 years of treating and transporting people to the hospital, I am a new recruit in a new position. A single role paramedic, or as I say, a single "roll" paramedic (a bagel), I want to share with you some of the fun and uplifting stories from over this first year of bagel probation.

SEPTEMBER 20, 2016
Tuesday

TODAY WAS MY FIRST DAY BACK at Station 6 where I have been working for the past few months before enrolling at the academy. Back then, I was working with Mike who was an excellent firefighter and paramedic. I learned a great deal from him but he got a new job with a bigger fire department and is no longer working here. I will miss him but today I have a new partner who is also very good and I am looking forward to working with and learning from her. She was just promoted from a single role paramedic to a firefighter-paramedic.

At Station 6, we work a "tour" of 48 hours. In comparison, a "shift" is made up of 24 hours. That is how they work here: 48 hours on and 96 hours off. Most people like the schedule but six months ago when I started as a temp, I didn't know if I could work that kind of schedule anymore. In my younger years, I had no problem with those kinds of hours. I regularly worked 72 hour shifts and once, I even worked a 120 hour shift. To my surprise, I am indeed able to work 48 hours straight and having four days off in a row is great.

Station 6 is on the edge of the district so if other medics from other stations are out on calls, we move to the center of the district to help field new incoming calls for their area. Many people don't like this move, but I don't mind. I have been stuck in an ambulance for so many years that I am happy to take their calls knowing I have a home station to go back to whenever we're cleared.

Today we had to field two calls from another station as well as drilling with the volunteers for two hours in the morning and for another hour in the evening. The first call was for a motor vehicle crash which came in while we were training with the volunteers in the morning. One of the interesting things about responding to a motor vehicle crash is that before we respond, we have to put on our "turnout gear"—boots and pants we also call bunkers. Though I'm not exactly sure where the term comes from, I think it's from the old days when the boots and pants were placed next to the firefighter's bunk for easy access for whenever a call came in during the middle of the night. That's what my dad, a volunteer firefighter and fire chief for 15 years, told me and I am sticking to that because my dad was awesome.

The vehicle crash was a rear end collision and one of the passengers was complaining of pain everywhere throughout her body. Though it was a low-impact crash, she wanted to go to the hospital so we took her in for an evaluation.

Other calls we received earlier in the day were medical calls. On medical calls we generally just wear our uniforms and no bunker gear so there's less preparation. My first patient was a little old lady who was standing on her chair doing a house chore, lost her balance, and fell. She struck her hip on the way down and she was in a lot of pain. We gave her medication for the pain and took her to the hospital. One of the treatments we can provide for patients is to relieve their pain and when I gave her two doses of the medication, she was so appreciative. "I feeeel beeeetter already," she said with a smile. She was such a kind woman and we had a nice talk on the way to the hospital.

In order to prevent fatigue, you always have two paramedics on a medic unit so you can switch back and forth between calls so my partner took the one after the older woman.

By the time we got back to the station, it was around 10:00 p.m. and I was ready to eat a meal then go to sleep. Out of the freezer, I took a frozen dinner I'd brought with me and heated it up in the microwave. It was, oh, so good: turkey, potatoes, and dressing with gravy. Hot and yummy and comforting. It's funny to think that a frozen dinner can be so delicious but after a long day in an ambulance taking calls, it felt like Thanksgiving dinner!

Hug your family before you go to sleep. Listen to and love your friends and family.

SEPTEMBER 21, 2016
Wednesday
GOOD MORNING.

We made it through the night without a call or a move up to another district. Amazing.

Despite the delicious frozen dinner I had last night, I need to be more organized with my meal planning here. All I had for breakfast was water and a Rice Krispy Treat before having to go to drill. Not exactly a well-balanced meal.

This morning's drill was great. To stay in practice for real calls, we have to go over various situations regularly so we know how to respond and work as a team. Today's practice was a fire drill going over strategies and tactics. After we completed the drill, I headed to the stockroom to gather the needed supplies to restock the medic along with the rest of the station. By the time I finished with that, it was time for lunch (leftovers) and then on to homework.

Have I explained the story behind this book's title? I was out at the drill site yesterday talking to the Battalion Chief when I told him I was a new recruit. He laughed and said, "No, you're not. You're a probie!" So begins the continuation of my 36 year career as a 63 year old probie. Have faith in yourself today. I am trying to have faith in myself.

♦♦♦

Tonight we had a late call. A student had been working out while already sick and dehydrated when he became lightheaded and vomited. We had him rest and drink water before he went home.

Nothing else happened for the rest of the night. Tonight I get to go home and rest in my own bed.

Countdown: 365 minus 2 days, only 363 more days of probation. Some days it is not easy to have faith, at least for me. Enjoy the day.

September 26, 2016.
Monday
This morning I started off the shift at a run. First, I had to write a turnover report, check for and obtain needed supplies from the storeroom, and then look over the condition of the medic. After fixing

and supplying all the missing items in the ambulance, I then gave it
a thorough washing before heading to our drill. Today we practiced
with air packs, a procedure I wasn't familiar with. However, while I
was watching and learning how to don the air pack, we received an
incoming medical call.

I generally take the first patient at the beginning of a shift. For
some reason, I have always done it this way and it seems to work well
at this station too. I mapped the address but everyone already knew
where we were going as the woman calls for an ambulance every week.
When we got there, she told us she had been vomiting for days on
end and wanted to go to the hospital. We quickly took her in to the
emergency department for evaluation before returning to the station
where I finished my report.

Part of being a recruit is keeping myself busy at all times. After
working the whole weekend in Portland, I am mentally tired. Though
I have four days off from being a probie, I fill in that time by working
medical standby in Portland as a second job so I really only have
one day off. Even then, I like to run volunteer calls for Mt. Angel
Fire when I'm home. Usually, I have great joy going on calls in Mt.
Angel. My dad was Fire Chief there and I know he would be proud
of me. Plus, many of the people I take care of knew me when I was a
child. It warms my heart to take care of these beloved people in my
community who both love and nurture me.

Back at our station, we had a cardiac arrest for a 37 year old man.
I got the endotracheal intubation (air tube) in and went in with the
crew to the hospital where I was relieved to know he was still alive.
It was a life-threatening case and I was so happy to have been part
of saving a life. (The person went home from the hospital three days
later with no neurological deficits!)

While we were at the hospital, my colleagues enjoyed giving me
a good-natured ribbing for being the oldest medic and probie at
MCFD#1. I didn't say much as helping the people around me feeds
my soul.

Today, I am once again reminded how lucky we all are with the gifts we are given every day. Despite the good-natured ribbing from my brothers, I hope I can continue to do this job for a long time to come. It's the job I have loved for so long, this lifelong career of taking care of people, showing respect and courtesy to all, and helping patients no matter their social or economic condition. This job is not for everyone. There's low pay, sometimes no pay, and I struggle with the fact that people usually have no understanding of my commitment to the poor and disenfranchised.

My hope for you today is that you seek out someone who needs your help and lend them a helping hand. So many say they *want* to help but never actually do it. They make statements about their beliefs yet don't put their money or actions behind them. Go buy someone shoes, clothes, or food. Just help—talk less and take more action.

Today I put out a call for *real* action—not words, but deeds. Give more and talk less. Allow your actions to talk louder than your words. Check on your neighbors and look out for them please. Show them kindness. Give to others.

September 27, 2016
Tuesday
Wow! It's been a busy morning.

This morning I went over the medic and put in new heart monitor batteries. Needing something to occupy myself with, I decided to try and take an edX class online. It's an eight hour class so I'm not done yet but I find it very interesting. I could not verify I took the class, though, since our station's computer doesn't have a camera with which to take my picture. When we go over to Station #1 after lunch, I'll see if they have a camera there and then I can work more on the class when we get back.

Because this is a slow station and I am a probie, I have to keep working and not sit around, even though, at some point, there is nothing else left to do. This afternoon the Battalion Chief stopped by for something, though I suspect he was also checking to see whether I was working or lounging around. I was working.

I am not sure how to explain my position here. I am the senior person when it comes to experience, yet the junior person when it comes to being new at the District. Though I have already worked six months as a temporary without the credit for it, I really don't know where I stand here.

Did I tell you I talked to two of the sleepers yesterday about keeping this place clean? It was a mess when I came in. Even at night, there are things needing to get done and it's not just probies who need to stay busy. We will see how it goes.

♦♦♦

I just finished the edX class and really enjoyed it. With that class completed, I've decided to spend more time taking additional self-paced courses to keep learning new things. Though sometimes I feel this culture doesn't want a 63 year old anything, my years of experience are appreciated here at MCFD#1. Yet, I still wonder—will they offer me opportunities to use these skills on special projects which will be good for me and be rewarding or will I just be that single role, the position very low in pay and often not respected? Everyone else wants to move to the firefighter-paramedic position but I'm happy simply being a paramedic and taking care of people. It bothers me when people forget to respect all positions and place so much emphasis on moving up to being a firefighter as if there is something wrong with doing a great job taking care of people as a medic, even as a single role paramedic.

Even without this respect or support, I am determined to develop my intellectual curiosity for things that stretch me as I have been stretched my entire career. For example, when I first started as a paramedic, in place of a heart monitor, we used a car battery and jumper cables. (Just joking!) Now we have 12 lead EKGs and I taught myself 12 lead interpretation. Working on and training myself on new technology stretches my mind and feels gratifying but what is the use? I feel old and not recognized for my abilities.

I know I have the ability to lead companies and make them successful but I know I will never get the chance. My deepest dream is to do a good job at whatever I'm engaged in. In my heart, I hold a commitment to excellence in everything I do, yet I have a sadness in my heart. Should I have done more with my life? How could I have done more? I suppose I should be thankful for what I *have* accomplished but the nagging question for me is, "Is it enough?" I just don't know.

◆◆◆

WE JUST GOT BACK TO THE station after three hours of calls and providing coverage for other stations.

One of the calls we received was a mutual aid call along with Woodburn Fire as no other ambulances were available in their area. I enjoy going up there and working with Woodburn Fire. They are incredibly nice to me. Knowing I have served for 36 years in EMS, they respect me for my longevity and depth of knowledge. Today they were so helpful and respectful. When we got there, their team had the patient all ready to go so I could administer pain medication before we had to move him. It is a gift to be able to relieve a person's pain and provide comfort. I gave the 93 year old man a large dose, double the regular amount, which, by protocol is only authorized if the medic can see the need and has the courage to think beyond the simple and make complex decisions. Critical thinking skills—the ability to reason and make educated decisions—are so important to have in this job. We loaded the patient into the ambulance and the Woodburn firefighters asked if I was full-time yet with MCFD#1. When I told them I was, they congratulated me and I added that the BC called me a probie, that I was the 63 year old probie! They chuckled since I've known most of them since they were children!

Lord, help me to serve and do my best. Grant hope to those who need hope and grace to those who need grace, hear them before they cry out in pain and suffering. Today, answer a prayer. Please, oh Lord, answer the prayer of those who suffer, answer their prayers today. (Job 14 rephrased)

It's 9:00 p.m. and I need to eat something before we get another call.

Please have faith in yourself, have faith in me, and let's have faith in the Lord together.

SEPTEMBER 30, 2016
Friday

I AM WORKING TODAY AT THE Portland Expo Center as I actually get paid more here than I do working for the county and I could use the money. While the Marion County Fire Department job is the worst paying job I have ever had, it's also the best job I have ever had. What? How? Why? I get to save lives, deliver babies, hold hands, and give comfort to those in crisis. Holding someone's hand who is frightened and afraid while reassuring them that it's all going to be okay is the best job a person can have in life. *And* I get to drive fast down the road in big red fire trucks and medics with red lights flashing and sirens blaring! Do you hear that? That's me with the siren clearing the way down the road getting to help others. How great!

OCTOBER

OCTOBER 2, 2016
Sunday

FOR THE LAST TWO DAYS I'VE been working medical standby in Portland at the Expo and Convention Centers. Going on at the same time was a lumber show and a wedding show. It made for a very interesting juxtaposition and there were a lot of interesting people to talk with and fun stuff to look at.

Today has been another great day for me. I'm working a 48 hour shift on Medic 33. It's Sunday and I have already checked out the medic and am looking forward to a nice, quiet day.

WELL, I SPOKE TOO SOON! WE are busy and have already responded to several calls.

Our first call was to help a mentally disabled person who had just experienced a 12 minute seizure. Though seizures are a normal part of the day or week for her, this seizure lasted too long so we took her to the hospital. Not wanting to put her through any more pain and suffering, I chose not to give her an IV, though, if she'd had another seizure, I would have given her IM medication. Even with her body contracted in a semi-permanent way, she still responded to my voice. It was such a sad situation.

There is so much going on in my own life that hurts my feelings and feels disruptive, just as I am sure you do in yours. Yet, we are lucky. We are fortunate to even have lives that are disrupted and interfered with by others. Lord, help me to appreciate what I have today. "Don't let the turkeys get you down," as the saying goes. Let's have hope. Yes, it *is* difficult to have hope some days. I know. I agree with and feel that sentiment myself.

We kept having calls all day long. The next one was for a man having chest pain. Blessedly, it was not a full STEMI (a heart attack where one of the arteries becomes blocked), but I think that it was a non-STEMI MI (a less severe and more common type of heart attack) and I completed the whole treatment plan myself. One of the first things I did was to give him fluid when his blood pressure dropped. He then had a moment of severe heart bradycardia (slow heart rate) and I used the "Victor jiggle" method to get him going again. I was relieved to see his heart rate come right back up and stay that way for the rest of the way to the hospital.

Our last call of the day was at midnight for a person having an anxiety attack who wanted a ride in to the hospital to get a shot as she had no other way to get there. Assessing the situation, though, I knew she didn't need a shot and that she had learned this was a way to get attention. So, speaking politely and courteously, I gave her words of comfort and spoke to her gently until she calmed down.

All told, in the first 24 hours of my shift, we had five transports and three coverages for the medic. It was not the quiet day I was expecting.

Tomorrow I meet with the Deputy Chief to find out about my class at UCLA and what the coverage will be for me for that class.

OCTOBER 3, 2016
Monday

THIS MORNING I GOT UP AND got myself ready for day two. The first thing I did was to check and restock the medic along with changing the batteries before making toast with butter and strawberry jam. We then drove down to Station 1 for a drill about building construction and fire suppression.

While there, I went up to talk to the Deputy Chief about taking the class at UCLA and found out that taking time off is not allowed for new employees. However, since I am taking time off for training purposes, he will allow me the time to go. I am now busy doing due diligence in trying to find trades for the days I need. We also looked at the days throughout the rest of the year that I'll need for highway safety training and he also talked to me about some plans of action he wants me to take. I'm relieved to know I still have a job.

After the training, we went out to Station 5 to work out at the training center. I did weights, the elliptical, stationary bicycle, and sit-ups. My partner spent the time running on the treadmill.

While I was changing by the medic back to my boots from my workout sneakers, a woman I know named Jillian came up to say hello. I had spoken to her the year before and encouraged her to pursue her dreams. She asked if I remembered her and I said yes. We were then joined by Mandi who is from Silverton Fire who did a case review with me last month. Both of them are taking the Emergency Medical Technician class. We talked for a while and I encouraged them to study their books diligently and to build a good foundation for their future by taking advantage of all their studies. I also got the chance to talk with Hadley who is in paramedic school. I really enjoy encouraging these young people, my "children" as I have been known to call the people I have encouraged, coached, and mentored over the years. It feels wonderful seeing them be so successful.

I am often reminded that compared to these young people, at 63 years old, I am not young. When I started this job, I told them I was 42 years older than the youngest person in the Academy and that none of them had been born yet when I got my NREMT Paramedic license in 1982. In a way, I find it a challenge to make it through the next year of probation—to become and stay strong, to be solid, as other people say, to have the mental and physical strength required and to then keep doing it day after day for many years to come.

I handed in my *verified* certificate of achievement for the Catalyst class on effective communication I completed last week through the edX system. I am pleased with myself that I completed the course and I learned something as well.

If you are reading this, then I somehow accomplished this year of probation. Right now, I don't know if I can complete the year. I have the faith, but I wonder if I have the strength. It is one thing to give strength and encouragement to others with a smile and a strong sense of urgency, it is quite another to fulfill it in oneself.

Have faith in yourself. Yes, I know that it is hard to have faith in oneself sometimes. I will try. You try too.

When I was a hospital chaplain at Memorial Hermann Hospital in Houston, Texas, there's a story I would often tell that comes from Isaiah 40:30-31. This is my paraphrase:

The children are exhausted and the people all give up.
Yet those who have HOPE in the Lord
Will receive new strength;
They will fly like eagles,
They will run and finish the race,
They will walk and not fall.

Hope and strength are commodities which are hard to come by on some days.

(In the Hebrew language, the most important item in a collection comes last. In English we generally place the most important thing first. That is where I take the above verses.)

THEY WILL FLY LIKE EAGLES

Anyone at any time can fly like an eagle if life is going great! Oh, yes. I have money, power, and control over everything and everyone and I am flying high in the sky. I am strong, independent, and secure while soaring like an eagle over life without a worry or care about anyone and anything else. As I said, this is listed first and people who speak the English language think this is the most important line. If life is easy for you, then you can soar through the heavens. However, when life is going great, this is easy for anyone.

THEY WILL RUN AND FINISH THE RACE

Life can be frustrating and you feel weak and unable to respond. You know you have to have faith and not give up. You need to finish the race. It's not easy having people ignore you. It's not easy to have your friends not stop, consider your condition, and help you overcome the situation. How do you finish the race then? All you need is for your perfect friends to consider your condition and help, but they don't help. They are fair-weather friends. I am sure you have seen this in your own life. Someone disagrees in a church and walks away taking others with them and leaving the church community devastated. Your poor friend needs help but *you* don't help. Somehow, they are not important and you are busy with the *important* friends. Status is more important than God's children. Who will help you finish the race, the insurmountable obstacle course? God will be there for you, look and see His footprints in the sand.

THEY WILL WALK AND NOT FALL

Life is overwhelming and you aren't going to make it to the finish line. You stumble and begin to fall. God will catch you. That is faith, a difficult faith to have at this very moment. Your friends are not here to help hold you up. The Lord is the only one who seems to love you and He *does* love you. He will not let you fall. *He will not let you fall.* You walk, you stumble, and you are weak and lonely and who is there for you?

The most important attribute is the last: God is there for you as you walk. Have you been abandoned by others? Have you seen rich churches, important people, people of influence, fail to help the poor and the needy? I have seen this many times. That is, unless they can get great press for their help. Let's all ask God to show us humility, love, and help for those who have nothing to give back to us. How about we help the poor among us, to actually take the time and come through for the promises you have made, to act without the expectation of reward or acknowledgement? Just step up and help.

Do you feel like you can't make it to the finish line? I do. I do not know how I will get there. If there is light at the end of the tunnel, that's great, but where is the tunnel? I cannot find the tunnel and only a mountain seems to stand in the distance. I have faith and hope, such as it is, and believe I will receive strength from the Lord. Today, let's feel the strength the Lord gives us. Then let's go help someone else as well without expectation of reward or acknowledgement.

♦♦♦

WE HAD THREE CALLS AFTER MIDNIGHT this shift. First, we had a repeat from last night's midnight call. This time, the woman could not sleep and she called to have us take her to the hospital because she needed a shot for her anxiety.

We had just returned from that call when we received a serious and strange one. A pair of security guards found an unresponsive young man in the grass and so they called 911. When we arrived, he was still out of it. Slow to respond with slurred speech and bumbling words, we could not understand anything he said. He did not know his name or birthday. His pupils were dilated and his tongue was green. My guess was that he had severe marijuana intoxication. I did all the right things: O2, IV, EKG monitor, CBG, and fluids.

After yet another call, we finally got back to the station around 6 a.m. to start a new day.

OCTOBER 8, 2016
Saturday
THIS HAS TURNED OUT TO BE a busy day as well. I started with checking and restocking the medic then working out for an hour before washing the medic and drilling until 2 p.m. After that, calls came in one after another until it was nighttime. Wow. No real rest or down time. I have the Portland Marathon in the morning and need to leave to get up there by 5 a.m. so Smoot is coming in extra early for me. Thanks.

OCTOBER 9, 2016
Sunday
I WAS AT THE PORTLAND MARATHON in the Medical Tent today and it rained the entire time. I have managed the critical medical area of the tent for many years.

OCTOBER 11, 2016
Tuesday
I ARRIVED TO THE STATION AT 6 a.m. this morning so Smoot would not get an early morning call and then get home late to find they had just returned from a 4:19 a.m. call. With another call coming in at 6:53 a.m., it's going to be a busy day.

Truly my soul finds rest in God; My salvation comes from him.

Psalm 62:1

♦♦♦

ANOTHER CALL JUST CAME IN FROM the rural area of the county for a man with cancer who was sick and needed to go to the hospital.

Overall, we've had a good shift. Many calls came in throughout the day. Among them was a two-year-old who was choking on a button who is now fine, someone in a vehicle that had rolled into a ditch, and lastly, a pregnant woman just released from jail.

The jail really aggravates me. It's in the middle of nowhere and when they release people, there is no way for them to get to town. There *is* a passing bus, if the person has money, but it seldom runs. I think it is cruel and unusual punishment for the people released who have nowhere to go and no way to get anywhere.

OCTOBER 15, 2016
Saturday

UNABATED, THE STORM FROM LAST NIGHT has grown in ferocity to the point there are predictions it will be another "Columbus Day"-like storm. When that storm happened back in 1962, I was eight years old. Despite the raging storm, I got started this morning cleaning up the kitchen and checking the medic then worked out at Station 5. We then had a meeting, drilled for two hours, and ate breakfast. So far, we've only had one call but there are lots of wires down and trees blocking the roads today.

I feel in a funk today after there was a big issue with my time off. I needed to know how to mark it on my time card and so I asked the Captain. He said I couldn't have any time off and no paid training time off either. I told him that it's time off without pay. It is like if someone was getting married—they would let you off. This was planned months ago and paid for by me. I hope I don't get into too much trouble asking him the question.

OCTOBER 20, 2016
Thursday

I AM AT THE CLEAR LAKE Station on Medic 33 today.

I have already checked the medic, queued up the computer so it's ready when we get a call, and swept the floor. Today is also the day we're wearing pink t-shirts for the month of October to promote cancer awareness.

I really like doing this job of taking care of people and am grateful to have the opportunity of working for MCFD#1. I hope I can make it through this probation period.

Now I am going to go wash the medic then head to drill.

Somehow, we just need to have faith in everything. I don't get it sometimes but we do need faith. Without faith, what do we have to hold on to, to give us strength and hope? I have perseverance and resilience. Yet, I wonder if my tank is getting low.

OCTOBER 21, 2016
Friday

GOOD MORNING. BY THE TIME WE got done yesterday with all the routine work and running out on calls, we didn't get back until late. We were then up at midnight for a call, another came in at 4:30 a.m., and yet another at 6:30 from out on the freeway, which ultimately was UTL.

When we finally got back from all of that, we had to quickly change into our official uniforms before rushing to a ceremony and fire drill. As soon as all that was done, another call came in to transport an older woman to the hospital. She'd been experiencing sudden hip and leg pain as well as low back pain. Though she told us she thought it was arthritis pain in her hip, I think it's a kidney stone. I gave her lots of pain medication with just a little pain relief.

Taking care of people really is the best job for me. I love working out of a fire station and being a member of a fire department.

I HAVE JUST BEEN ASKED TO come out to St. Paul Fire to work additional hours for them and I have said yes. It means a new set of ideas and ways of doing things as well as some extra income. I am told I will work at least two 24 hour shifts a month. So that, along with the OCC hours, should keep me busy. With 10 or more hours a week on average there, I should be working about 70 hours a week between all of my jobs.

Today I thought about all the information I am having to learn. How active my brain must be with all this new information to learn and remember! It feels like a continuous movement of throwing out old information and replacing it with new, important information. One of my colleagues told me today they have the same issue. They keep adding things and letting go of things that are not so important. For example, I no longer remember all of the 72,793 IVs I have started, the 17 babies I have delivered, or the many lives I have saved or the ones I haven't. I do remember a few, the ones which really grabbed me and stood out to me. That is how it is for everyone in life. One person remembers the ice cream cone and the other remembers the heat from the sun. What is significant to one person is not to another. The bully never remembers who they have hurt but the person they hurt remembers forever.

I believe we should be thankful for the good things we remember and even more thankful for the bad things in our lives that we don't. Some people hold onto hard feelings for decades. Why, I don't know. They become bitter and hateful. It is better to find peace and let go of the guilt, hurt, and misunderstandings.

Even so, some days it takes so much faith to just go forward. I don't fully understand it all and certainly don't have all the answers. But here is something I hold on to from Nahum 1:7, "The Lord is good, a refuge in times of trouble. He cares for those who trust in Him." Lord, I have faith and trust you. Help me to believe and trust in you more.

Victor 3 at Oktoberfest

November

November 2, 2016
Wednesday

TODAY IS THE SECOND DAY OF my shift. I just never had the chance to write yesterday so I am taking the opportunity now to update you on the time I was gone to training as well as my time here at work.

We had three calls after midnight at the end of our shift last week and were up the entire night. On Saturday, I slept and then gathered things together for my upcoming trip.

THE TRIP

THE TRAINING TRIP WAS AWESOME. I learned so many new things in the classes I took which is exactly why I went away for 48 hours of paramedic refresher training. I wanted to meet new people and hear new ideas—to see fresh faces and find out about different ways of seeing things.

Yesterday, an article I wrote was published in the Oregonian, both in the print version and online. I was so happy to see my words and ideas out there for the world to read and believe it can make a difference.

Here it is:

NOVEMBER 1, 2016 IN THE OREGONIAN
EVERYONE MUST WORK TOGETHER TO GET HOME SAFELY
VICTOR HOFFER

It is a difficult day when a fire chaplain comes knocking on your door or the trauma surgeon ushers you into a side room.

Your boy or girl is dead.

Both of my boys were in motor vehicle crashes. One boy survived his traumatic brain injury, and my other boy died.

Many of us have felt the heartbreak of death in our families or our friends' and neighbors' from traffic crashes. Highway safety advocates know the importance of life. We all want our sons, daughters, husbands and wives to come home to us each day. This year in particular has had many sad days on our highways and streets.

Pedestrian, bicyclist, motorcycle and car crash deaths and serious injuries have increased dramatically so far this year in Oregon. Compared to this time last year, our overall fatalities have increased by about 9 percent. Bicyclist deaths have nearly doubled, from 5 percent at this point last year to 9 percent in 2016.

It's critical that we put away the distractions and watch out for each other. In addition, on Nov. 6, we turn our clocks back one hour and darkness will fall on us even earlier. Let's get everyone home every night.

Drivers, please be watchful and attentive when driving. Keep an eye out for bicyclists and pedestrians. Drive carefully and stay alert to your surroundings. Bicyclists and pedestrians, wear white, bright and/or reflective clothing and stay alert.

Awareness is key, and focusing on safety is the way. Whether you are bicycling, driving, walking or riding a motorcycle, you need to focus on the task at hand and not allow distractions that, in a split second, can result in death.

We can all work together, one day at a time, to get everyone home safe in our communities. Safety advocates are asking everyone to continue to be vigilant about highway safety, especially as we head into the holiday season. Don't drink and drive. Buckle up yourself and your children properly. Slow down, don't hurry and plan your trip. Watch out for each other.

Drivers, pedestrians, bicyclists and motorcyclists can all work together—and must work together—to be safe on our roads and make it home to our families and friends during this holiday season and all year long.

Victor Hoffer is a resident of Mt. Angel and chairman of the Oregon Transportation Safety Committee. He's also a paramedic with Marion County Fire District #1 and volunteers with the Mt. Angel Fire District.

I told the Captain about the article when it was published and got into trouble for not asking permission to say I worked for MCFD#1.

TODAY, WE WERE BUSY WITH CALLS and drills. Then at midnight, a man and woman drove up to the station in their truck needing first aid. I jumped up into the medic to open the bay door and rushed her onto the stretcher so we could use the light inside. Since it was my partner's turn, he took care of this patient.

As it turns out, the woman had taken a pill given to her by a friend a couple of nights ago to help her sleep and it gave her a rash. Tonight she took another one and was now red all over her body. For this allergic reaction, my partner treated her with Benadryl. I believe that it was a niacin flush as I've seen many of these over the years. Except for her being red and flushed, she had no other medical problems.

This morning we treated someone with an anxiety problem who stopped taking her medication so we treated her by convincing her to take some of her pills and make an appointment with her doctor. She asked if I would pray for her so I told her my favorite Charles Wesley story about having trust in the storm when you're in the middle of the fierce winds and she seemed relieved.

WE JUST RETURNED FROM A CALL for an older woman with a breathing problem who probably has pneumonia. I treated her with oxygen along with a duo neb and she felt better. It doesn't seem that she's well taken care of by her family and I don't think they have the skills to take care of her to the degree that she needs help. Having taken care of Mom the last two years before she died, I appreciate how lucky we were to be able to take care of her at home with us and in great surroundings.

We also had a late night call come in from Hallelujah Drive. I knew exactly where we were going and as we approached the house, my partner told me to drive by the entrance. She was mapping it on a device and thought the entrance was in a different location. When we got to 54th Street, I told her the entrance was behind us. She yelled at me and said, "Go ahead then if you know where you're going!" I promptly turned around and went directly to the address. She later apologized.

When we arrived, we found an elderly lady on the floor who was having a syncopal episode (lost consciousness) and were told she was on hospice. If someone is on hospice, we are not allowed to take them to the hospital. While I was talking with the hospice nurse, our captain arrived and we lifted the woman off the floor and into a soft chair. The woman's daughter then arrived and the captain was trying to explain the treatment options available for her mom which the daughter was not understanding. I could see the problem and so stepped in to explain what he meant in a way she could comprehend in such a crisis moment and we decided to help Mom into her bed instead. Though a caregiver was already there to take care of her, they needed more help so we arranged for a nurse to come out as well. I'm glad we were able to be there for them.

The really interesting things that happened were *around* the call. As it turned out, the husband of the patient was a retired pastor. When I told him I attended Southern California College (now Vanguard University) and that, while there, I was the Senior Pastor Intern for Dr. George Wood, he told me he was also a SCC alumni and he was amazed because he knows Dr. Wood as the General Superintendent of the Assemblies of God and, in fact, regularly sees him at the Assemblies of God Annual General Assembly. After we completed his wife's treatment, I told him two stories about my time at SCC. (For background information, for the Assemblies of God, the General Superintendent is like the Pope.)

I told them that after church on Sunday we would go to Pastor Wood's house for the afternoon to talk, rest, eat, and watch football. In the evening, we would leave to eat dinner at the college cafeteria before heading back to church for the evening service and that he would always walk us to the door. This one time, though, he didn't get up to walk us to the door like he usually did. He just waved from the sofa and said goodbye. I was so worried that he was angry with me for some reason. The very next week we were there again and so was Dad Wood. Dad Wood was Pastor Wood's dad and was a devoted and hardworking missionary from his younger years all the way through until he retired and moved close to his son. When Dad Wood got up and announced he and his wife were leaving, Dr. Wood looked up and waved goodbye without getting up. Wow! After Dad Wood had gone, I asked why he didn't walk him to the door like he did everyone else. He replied, "I don't walk family to the door." Oh my gosh, I wasn't in trouble, I was family!

I then told the daughter, who had joined the conversation, about the first time I met George, Dr. Wood's son. I was teaching George's first grade Sunday school class and he was misbehaving like any kid does. When I told him to sit down, he retorted that he didn't have to, that his dad was the pastor. I looked straight into his eyes and said, "I don't care, sit down." He promptly sat down and became my biggest fan over the next two years before I graduated from college. George must be in his 40s now.

I believe the family of our patient felt relieved to know a person with similar beliefs and familiar friends was the one treating their wife and mother and I told them it was a privilege to take care of the children of God. I am thankful for not only the opportunities I've had to help people over the last 36 years, but now to also get to work for MCFD#1.

I am still very worried about my position. I received an email today from the Deputy Chief to come talk to him about my special leave time away from the job for the UCLA class. I am happy to not be paid but there *are* rules for being off during probation. He may tell me I won't be allowed the time off and I am afraid of that as I need this time off to work on highway safety and attend the meetings. I am still hoping to be able to trade shifts, though, so far, I haven't found any takers. What do I do now? I hope I will be able to get trades but so far, I've had no cooperation from colleagues on any trades. I guess if they let me go, they let me go. Getting all the moms and dads, boys and girls home every night is more important to me than any one job. I could work at a store and make almost as much as the $12.23 an hour I am getting for saving lives and delivering babies.

I am at the Oregon Convention Center and just saw an Oregon State Trooper I know who is serving on security detail for the Governor. The Governor is here for the benefit dinner at the OCC and Jay Leno is the featured speaker so there is a lot of security and a lot of people attending the benefit. The trooper told me she has 17 months until retirement though she seems young. I told her I had

10 months until I get off of *probation*. She smiled at that and wished me luck. She was always a great person to work with at the Oregon State Fair and on the highways at crashes.

Talking with her brought me back to the question of why I'm at this place in my journey at this time in my life. Why are my many talents not recognized and utilized? And how have I come this far in my career only to worry about being fired at the lowest paying job possible? Though it's low paying, it's also one of the most important jobs—saving lives—and that means something to me. Being involved in the community is important to me.

We may be standing on the solid rock, but the storm is still blowing around us. The rain is pouring down and the waves are crashing against our bodies. "Have faith!" I have said in one of my two favorite sermonettes while at Memorial Hermann Hospital in Houston. For that talk, I spoke about Matthew 7:24-27 and how one family survived and one did not survive. I will share the talk later but for now, I just want to say that I hear my words but it is just so difficult to continually get punched in the face by the rain and the wind and the waves and yet have hope and faith. Even the solid rock feels the force of the storm, the erosion of the relentless impact of the rain and wind and waves. My heart is heavy and sad tonight.

Semper paratus, always ready.

Old, rough and ready.

I stopped at the fire station on my way to the GAC on DUII on Friday morning. It was the second day of my shift at Station 1. The medic was just backing in from running a call and the admin office was not open yet so I went over to the station to say hello and sign my payroll sheet.

The crew were there doing their morning talk so I told Captain Smith I was signing my payroll sheet with Anita and was also looking for the Deputy Chief. When I shared with him I was worried I was going to get fired, he laughed and said not to worry until I was being told to meet with the Chief, Deputy Chief, Battalion Chief, and

Captain. Captain Smith is a wonderful officer; he is both smart and provides good leadership to his crew and the entire team.

I believe the fire crew respects and likes me and they seem genuinely glad I'm there as a medic. By the time I get done with probation in a year, I will be the senior single medic. We all chuckled about how fast singles test out to firefighter status. A test *is* coming up in January and all the other four from my Academy will test to become firefighters.

I then saw the Fire Chief and said hello. He has an open door policy and it's nice to be able to visit for a minute and just say hi to him. While there, I gave him a copy of the safety article and he was very pleased that MCFD#1 was acknowledged.

While watching a little TV and resting on Thursday, I came up with two personal themes for me in addition to being a probie. The first one is the USCG motto of *Semper Paratus,* which means *always ready* and due to my age, maybe *"Old Rough and Ready,"* the nickname for President Zachary Taylor. He got the nickname because of his willingness to share the hardships of field duty with his men. It seems he understood the difficulties the Native American Indians were going through and tried to protect them by stopping the settlers' encroachment into Native American Indian lands.

At the DPSST GAC DUII meeting, Annette, the Executive Assistant, was ill and couldn't be there so I stepped in to make announcements. I first gave a brief report from the OTSC reminding members they were invited to the January Silver Falls Highway Safety meeting at Silver Falls State Park then shared that the TSAP was approved by the Commission and sent to the US Department of Transportation.

After the meeting, I just had enough time to run home and change into my fire clothes before taking the fire rescue truck to the high school to escort the John F. Kennedy High School cross country team out of town on their way to the state finals! The cross country team was so excited. One girl, Ortiz, asked if she could climb onto the rescue and I said yes. She immediately climbed into the back seat and I asked if she wanted to climb on top. "Yes!" she exclaimed. So she climbed up and the whole team followed! The parents got pictures of the team on top of the rescue and everyone was happy and excited. Some of the boys and girls were so funny as they climbed back down the ladder. "I am afraid of heights." They shouted out in glee as they looked down. Still, I had one boy guard them as they came down with me ready below to catch anyone who might miss a rung or freeze up. Ortiz, who started at the high school this fall, came up to hug me and said, "Thank you!" while I was talking to the parents. It was sweet and she was so polite.

Our plan was to then escort the students to the middle school with the sirens and air horn blaring and the red lights flashing. Everyone loves red lights and sirens! As everyone piled onto the minibus and vans, I spotted Ortiz and asked her if she wanted to ride in the rescue. She leaped into the front seat and found great delight in running the siren and air horn as we blared through downtown on our way to the middle school. Once there, everyone hopped out and gave the students high fives before I escorted them to the city limits. As we pulled out of the middle school's parking lot, the boys were pulling their arms in the "blow the air horn sign" and we blared our way out

of there. Huge smiles all around. At the edge of town, I pulled to the side so they could go around me and you could see and feel their excitement. Hands were waving, car horns sounding, and my rescue siren just blaring as loud as can be! How much fun that was to see happy parents and happy children!

Everyone, hug your children and your grandchildren. Do it today! Buy food for the neighbor who needs a little help. Understand that some people are having a difficult time today and will not tell anyone. Go forward and seek out someone to show kindness whether in a small or big way.

> *I pray that the eyes of your heart may be enlightened in order that you may know the hope to which he has called you.*
> *Ephesians 1:18*

Please seek out someone to help today. When I was in seminary, we were very poor but didn't tell anyone. Some people *do* ask for help. At church one Christmas, another seminary student stood up and said he was really struggling financially. A parishioner then gave the pastor $300 for them which would be around $1,000 today. It was very kind of the parishioner but there are others who won't tell you they need help. For example, we decided to trust God for what we needed. Though we worked hard and paid all our bills, at the end of the day, we had very little left. On Christmas Day, we had food for our three year old and a dollar left over for us. With that, we bought a one dollar pizza and that is what we had for Christmas along with a handmade gift. We just never said anything. That time made me realize that even when it comes to food baskets, it's the people with transportation and gas money who have the ability to go pick one up. Will you *please* find someone to help, please?

NOVEMBER 5, 2016
Saturday

TODAY I'M AT THE PORTLAND EXPO Center doing first aid for Girlfest 2016. There are *thousands* of girls running around, thousands of Girl Scouts in one place. It's overwhelming and delightful and rather like an indoor-outdoor camp. All the girls are earning badges from different activities inside the hall. I am stationed outside in the foyer across from where the bathrooms are located. You can imagine how many Scout Leaders and moms are taking the girls to the bathroom. The place is a loud roar. Where I'm stationed, my door is a split level door and some of the girls lean over to say hello so I get up to return their greeting. They quickly spot my Tinker Bell sticker on the back of my name badge and I tell them I'm Tinker Bell's uncle. The Scout mom laughs at this and so I offer them Tinker Bell dust. (Now I usually only use this for little children who are hurt and need a distraction for which it works very well.) They all wanted the Tinker Bell dust and after they left, one of the moms came back over and asked to have some as well. She looked just like a kid squatting down for her dust! I am now going to have to call Tink to get more dust as I am almost out! To me, showing kindness to others to brighten their day is easy and a great thing to do. They may only go home with one badge but they will all have some Tinker Bell dust to make them happy and help their day along.

NOVEMBER 6, 2016
Sunday

I WAS CALLED IN TO WORK for a sick firefighter-medic. He was sick and went home as soon as I arrived at Station 2. They had already transported two people and we ended up running calls all day long and into the evening. I didn't sleep well at all as we kept getting calls so I was tired in the morning.

On an aside, another medic called me to ask if I could trade a shift with him. I said yes to working for him on the 18th and he picked Tuesday to cover for me. This is great as I won't have to take special leave for my OTSC meeting. (The meeting went well and I was reelected as Chair for 2017.)

NOVEMBER 7, 2016
Monday

THE DAY WAS BUSY—WE HAD SEVEN calls with four of those calls coming from Woodburn for mutual aid to Woodburn Fire.

The first call was a MVC. When we arrived, the Fire Chief of Woodburn Fire was also helping and it was nice to see him as I've known him for many years. We transported a woman to Salem Hospital Emergency but I don't believe she was injured. She said her hip and flank hurt and so she wanted to go to the hospital but on the ride there, she spent the whole time resting and sleeping, exhibiting no pain response whatsoever.

Then around 4 a.m., we got a call to I5, the freeway we cover from our station. It was very foggy and difficult to see the roadway as we raced down the road with red lights and sirens. The call was for a person along the side of the freeway. We could see the fire engine ahead of us and we were a half mile behind them. I spotted the person on the side of the freeway and yelled for my partner to stop. As soon as we pulled over, I ran to the person and saw he had been hit by a car, probably at 60 plus mph, and was dead on impact. I pronounced him dead at the scene and informed our dispatch. As the Oregon State Police have jurisdiction there, I was going to wait for them but the Battalion Chief told me we didn't need to wait for them as the fire truck was there by then.

NOVEMBER 8, 2016
Tuesday

I FINALLY GOT TO LIE BACK down at 5 a.m. Though I thought about just shaving, showering, and getting ready for the OTSC meeting, I just couldn't. I had to rest my brain. Once again, a person had been lost to a traffic crash. Regardless of whether the man was homeless, a transient, or a hitchhiker, someone is sad today having lost a father or a friend. You know that I believe in Outcome Zero®, a belief in reducing traffic deaths to none at all. My take is to do this *one day at a time* by doing my part to get everyone home each day and to then string those one days into many connected days. I am grieving that today is not one of those days.

This isn't just a saying or motto for me. It's personal. I lost my son, brother, and dad all to traffic crashes and I no longer have them here to enjoy life with me. Every time I lose a person, every time I am there to look into their sad, hazed-over eyes and tell them, "I am sorry there is nothing I can do for you," and pronounce them dead, I think of all the grief of those who love them and I feel painfully sad.

My symbol for "Outcome Zero: One Day at a Time" ®

November 14, 2016
Monday

It's been a very busy two days and only now at 9 p.m. on day two have I had time to sit down and work on my "star date log."

Ever since I arrived for my shift, we've had calls, I've worked on projects, took part in drills, and did research for my talk on Saturday. Oh my goodness! I am so tired. It certainly didn't help that I arrived home at 1 a.m. on Sunday from doing a standby at the Keller and then went to work only four hours later.

Thus far, we've had one fire call, a MVC, several very sick people, and my last call was a seizure patient who has not yet woken up. No one knows what is wrong with her. She is very ill and only 36 years old. It's sad in so many ways.

Just as I was sliding into my chair to write this tonight, my chair tipped over landing me hard on the floor. Though it's kind of funny, my side, back, and shoulders hurt. Now I'm listening to Christmas music as it gives me hope and the funny and serious song combinations make me smile through the hurt.

Today I'm reminding myself that I generally do not understand the way things go for people, myself included. So for tonight I will go to sleep after finishing my talk and ponder this: "God's voice thunders in marvelous ways; he does great things beyond our understanding." Job 37:5

November 20, 2016
Sunday

Hello. What a weekend shift! We have been extremely busy. On Friday, I worked Medic 32 for a coworker who needed the day off. He worked for me last week on my OTSC day and I am happy we switched though we were busy with calls and other projects all shift long.

First, we went to cover Medic 33 for a drill then went down to Station 5 to help put out barrels for the MCFD#1 food drive at Clear

Lake School. I was impressed that the Fire Chief was there with his work gloves carrying barrels and directing the effort.

While there, Chief Riley came up and told me he'd met with the MCFD#1 Board of Directors and had presented the article I wrote for the Oregonian along with the letter from Matthew Garrett, the Director of ODOT. He proudly told me that on behalf of the Board of Directors, "Congratulations on your hard work for highway safety!" He had a great big smile on his face. I was so thankful.

After we distributed the barrels, we went to a drill, and were then busy with calls for the rest of the shift, eight in total, including two after midnight.

On Saturday, we had breakfast and drill. M33 and E305 were responsible for the breakfast this week. We each put in ten dollars a month for the two breakfasts we eat on our Saturday duty days. It was my turn to teach today and I spoke on Cannabinoid Hyperemesis Syndrome. I think I did okay. It was a tough crowd. I know from experience to limit my talk to about 10 minutes as after that, you begin to lose your audience. After we attended to several calls, I finally got a short nap after having been up all night.

THIS MORNING WE TOOK A MAN in severe respiratory distress to the hospital. His initial oxygen saturation was 66% with five LPM on his CPAP device. I gave him oxygen through a nasal cannula, nebulizer, and our CPAP, and managed to get his saturation up to 90%. His wife told me he is very ill with cancer and she also mentioned that MCFD took in her niece last week for seizures. She was talking about the woman I took in!

Thank you Lord for helping me with all the people I get to take care of as a medic. It challenges me to make them better and to be kind to them. "Your word is a lamp for my feet, a light on my path." Psalm 119:105

There was another call of particular interest from the recovery center for a very sick woman who is also an alcoholic. I took care of her and was my normal self, I think, as I showed her respect, courtesy, and understanding. I started an IV and gave her a fluid bolus to help make her feel better and as we arrived at the hospital, she thanked me. For a moment I was confused. She said thank you for being nice to her. I was astounded, though not too surprised. I suspect that many medics are rude. They treat her like she is a bad person, rather than someone in need of help and understanding. She then asked me if I knew a certain medic from Salem. I did! He is a local boy and I know his parents as well. I asked her to pass on my regards to him. So the morals of the story are numerous. First and foremost, treat all people with respect, courtesy, and show understanding no matter their condition or circumstances. This person is sick and is trying to get better. A little respect goes a long way. Second, you never know who you are talking to when you are taking care of someone. Showing a little love and respect makes such a difference. Just be kind in what you do and how you see people.

NOVEMBER 24, 2016
Thursday – Thanksgiving Day
I'M WORKING TODAY AT STATION 1 and have already had a call, checked out the medic, restocked it, restocked the station EMS kiosk, and changed the main oxygen tank.

On Tuesday, I worked at the OCC. It was fun as it was the last day of a science symposium and I had plenty of blisters, upset stomachs, and one person who needed to rest because he felt weak. The people were all very smart, PhD types, and it was enjoyable interacting with them.

Yesterday, I was very sick. The flu shot I got last week must have given me the flu so I just drank a lot of fluids and didn't eat so I could feel better for today's holiday.

This is me on Thanksgiving at Station 1.
Thursday, November 24, 2016

Yes, today is Thanksgiving and I am working Medic 31. Patti made stuffing for me and just delivered it to the station.

> *Enter his gates with thanksgiving and courts with praise; give*
> *thanks to Him and praise His name. For the Lord is good and*
> *His love endures forever; His faithfulness continues through all*
> *generations.*
>
> *Psalm 100:4-5*

For Thanksgiving, we went down to Station 2 to make dinner. The stuffing was great! I waited for everyone to get their food before getting mine. I had just placed it in the microwave to heat it up when we got a call to assist Engine 10.

Oh my goodness, a little girl had knocked a pot of hot chocolate off the stove and badly burned herself. We arrived on scene and carried her to the medic where I started an IV. It was a 24 gauge needle and worked great, the hospital was even able to draw blood from it. To help her pain, I gave her two doses of Fentanyl. The medic who rode in with me asked if I wanted to give a second dose of Fentanyl and if we should call the hospital for advice. I didn't think we needed to call the hospital as we know what to do along with what to watch for and so I gave her more pain medication. She looked far more comfortable after that—if anyone that badly burned could even begin to be comfortable. I estimated her body was 11% burned. Her hand was sloughing off skin. Ouch, very painful!

After we returned to the station, I microwaved my food and enjoyed my dinner! I have completed my chart now and sent it on to the hospital before getting to rest for a minute.

I am thankful to be here at Marion County, to get to continue to help others, to be appreciated by my colleagues, and to see my friends at the hospital.

Please pray for your friends and family and be kind to everyone. Be particularly kind to those in need and help someone today. Make someone feel appreciated and special.

Earlier in the day, we had the critically burned girl who was transferred to Emanuel Burn Center and now we have a baby! As soon as we received a call for an impending birth, we raced to the house but while we were still en route, we were notified the baby had been delivered and CPR was in progress. When we arrived and rushed into the home, we found the baby on Mom's belly, barely breathing and cyanotic. Quickly, we cut the cord and I started resuscitating the child. Seaton soon arrived and we went out to the ambulance to dry the infant off and continue resuscitation while my partner stayed inside to care for the mother. After drying off the infant and stimulating her in an attempt to get her to breathe, I listened to her lungs and measured a heart rate of 94 so we kept working. I gave the hospital early notification we were soon coming in with a mom and baby and that my partner would give an update when we began our transport. The engine crew got the mom loaded into the ambulance and I drove what we call "Code 3," which is red lights flashing and sirens sounding all the way to the hospital.

Though it was truly a life and death situation, I was quick and careful as there are lots of ambulance crashes in the United States each year and I am careful not to be one of the statistics. As I was driving, I was reminding myself I had the lives of five people in the back of my medic. Arriving safely at the hospital with the baby now breathing, we delivered the baby and her mother directly to Labor & Delivery. The mom was fine and the baby pinked up for us and was also doing fine. As we walked through the doors, a nurse called the mom by name and so I questioned her, "How do you know her name?" The nurse replied that the mom was at the hospital earlier in the day and they had sent her home!

I have now delivered 17 babies in my career as a medic. This one doesn't count, however, as we weren't there for the actual delivery but we did cut the cord and, most importantly, resuscitated the baby! So as in football when it is a team effort to get a tackle and a person is credited with half a tackle, I am going to give myself half a "tackle" and count 17.5 deliveries in my career! (Down at UCLA, I met a medic who had delivered 300 babies. He was in an interesting part of Los Angeles for most of his career but for most medics, 17.5 is a lot of babies.)

November 25, 2016
Friday

It is 5:30 p.m. and we are finally back from holding out boots for a fundraiser and I just finished two charts. Outside, it's cold and overcast with rain coming down but holding that boot out for people was sure fun!

So far today, I have 13,531 steps in. We came back to Station 6 so the crew could have a break and get lunch. We then ran a call to the Lutheran Home just up the street to help a sick lady with what smelled like a severe UTI, then helped a poor alcoholic who was cold, wet, and hungry who wanted to go to the hospital.

The fun and interesting call of the day was for a 96 year old lady who was getting her hair done when she sat under the dryer for too long and passed out. This woman was taking metoprolol which keeps your heart from pumping too hard and fast and so while sitting in one place for so long, blood had pooled in her legs and the heat warming her head was just too much for her. She needed a little more blood to her head so I used the Victor jiggle method and she woke right up and was fine. After going over everything with her, I stood her up, danced with her, and she was feeling great. I then arranged for a ride home for her from the beauty shop and that was that for the call.

I want to share with you something I have said before but that needs reiterating. When you see a medic, thank them for their service. I saw a colleague at the hospital and he's having a difficult time coping with the stress of the job. We are out here helping people because that is what we truly believe in deep in our hearts but there are some people who make it so hard for us.

For me, I think about how much fun I've had the last two days getting to really help people and I smile. First, I treated the girl with the burn and loaded her up with pain medication. Then, there was the baby delivery and making sure she survived a home birth without anyone attending to her. Lastly, today I helped several other people—souls who needed help. Then to finish it up, I was out on the street with a boot raising money for a good cause and people gave generously. Fun.

What truly frustrates me are not the patients but those in private ambulance management who are often only there for the bottom line and who are making too much money at the expense of the paramedics. The paramedics who work for such companies are often severely underpaid while having to sit in ambulances on street corners while waiting for calls in order to save money for the company. I am sure we will all have cancer someday from idling our diesel ambulances and breathing in all those fumes. It sure is making people at the top lots of money but it is killing careers, backs, and the good intentions of the paramedics on the street.

As you know, I have been doing this for 36 years now and I still love what I do each day. Of course, I wonder if I should have been a tough and hard-fisted lawyer with lots of money and fame. Being mean is not me, though. I want to be kind, understanding, never to attack another, but to be patient and peaceful in disagreement. In my career, I have seen 70,000 plus patients and double or triple that in family members of patients so that's at least 250,000 people. I have made it a habit to toss everything out of my mind after it occurs. I think that is how I have survived the horrors of EMS. Now my friends from Salem Fire greet me when they see me on a call as does Woodburn Fire as I mentioned earlier. I think that shows true kindness and genuine respect from them for my experience, knowledge, medic skills, and critical thinking abilities. It means everything to me.

While waiting for another call, I was sitting and trying to rest my brain and body for a few minutes. Sitting there, I suddenly had an overwhelming case of sadness and I was brimming over with sorrow. In my heart, I spoke to my son, Victor 3, to tell him how much I missed him. I then told Dad the same thing and shared with them both how I was sorry for any and all my failings in relation to them. Even with talking it out in my heart, I just couldn't break the sense of sorrow so I texted my other son, Paul, and my wife, Lynell. Sixty-three years old and it felt like my heart had a mind of its own that I couldn't stop. I decided to try lying down for a nap instead. I have tried my best for everyone in my life. I suppose I fail more than succeed, though I keep trying.

> *And whatever you do, whether in word or deed, do it all in the name of the Lord Jesus, giving thanks to God the Father through him.*
>
> *Colossians 3:17*

I guess I will keep trying.

November 26, 2016
Saturday

I am so tired. With 48 hours down and 24 to go here at the station, I still have an 8 hour shift in Portland on Sunday. This morning I got up early to shave, shower, and get dressed in my uniform and badge. I then cleaned the kitchen, emptied the garbage, and headed to Station 2 for our breakfast and training. The smell of biscuits and gravy wafting from the kitchen smelled so good but before we could sit down to eat, a call came in from the dialysis center for a man who fell.

Engine 305 was already on the scene by the time we got there and had the scoop stretcher ready to move the patient. A firefighter-medic I work with named Mike Berger was one of the other responders and I like him. He is smart, competent, and always direct. Together we got the poor guy off of the floor and onto the stretcher where he immediately felt better. Of course, anything is going to feel better when you've been lying on a hard, cold floor. With him was a large wheelchair that everyone else wanted to leave behind for someone to retrieve later but after I got him into the medic, I went back in and said, "No, we will take the wheelchair. If he goes home from the hospital, he will appreciate being in his own wheelchair that fits him and is definitely more comfortable than the standard chairs the transport company carries." I believe it's important to not only look out for a patient's safety, but for their comfort as well.

While hopping back into the medic, my partner told me the patient knows me and my dad. Wow. Dad has been gone for 25 years come December 17th and Victor 3 died on January 2, 2009. I didn't know what to say. It seems like yesterday and forever all at the same time. He had seen my Hoffer name on my uniform and so we had a brief talk about my dad. Feeling quite weak, he rested for the rest of the way to the hospital.

We headed back after that to the meeting at the station where breakfast had already been served and consumed. The meeting and training were all but over but I managed to find a beautifully burnt biscuit and some leftover gravy. We then headed up to Station 1 for supplies and to clean up the MDA items. Finally, we got to go back home to Station 6 where we got a call.

The call was for a patient I saw last week. He had just returned home from the hospital where they signed him up for hospice. Hospice had come out to fill out the paperwork but didn't give the wife any help or suggestions on how to take care of him. She is completely overwhelmed. The reason we were called was to help him off of the toilet because he didn't have the strength to do it and she couldn't lift him. It is a total and complete failure on the part of the hospital and the hospice agency. They should have thought ahead and predicted the outcome of sending him home without assistance. He needs nursing home care or in-home care. Hospice just signed the papers and left. The hospice agency assigned to them is not my favorite. This man has been taken off of all his medications and is going to die very soon. It's absurd! Ridiculous! Such a lack of care will not only hasten his death, it will kill him. But it will save the insurance company lots of money.

We ran our last call around 2:00 in the morning then came back to get some sleep. This morning I'm heading to Portland to work at the Expo Center and I'm looking forward to it. Brian is so kind and supportive. Good morning.

December

December 1, 2016
Thursday

I am at Station 6 on Medic 33 today. I have already checked out the medic and am temporarily at Station 1 for an Honor Guard practice for my partner. I need to call the Fire Chief of St. Paul Fire today and tell him I can't work for him right now. I really want to go out there and help but I just feel like that would be too much for me with so much else going on at this time.

One thing I really want to do is to write the stories of my career that stand out in my mind of people pleading, "Please don't let me die," but I am feeling overwhelmed right now. I accepted three additional shifts from MCFD yesterday for December. That gives me 15 shifts total or 360 hours at County. I am also working medical support for three days at the Expo Center in the first half of December. Though I am already so busy, I took the extra shifts so someone doesn't get a mandatory call back.

Finally, I wanted to tell you I watched a wonderful Dolly Parton special last night about her life and Christmas. She had a very difficult childhood. So, again, I am asking you to go out and find someone who could use a little something. Maybe it will be obvious to you or maybe you will need to find those three boys who look like a handful for their mother and just bless them with love and gifts. Maybe you can give them food, clothes, or a warm coat. Try to find the good in the children and not judge anyone. Find peace and love in people, not judgment.

"Give thanks to the Lord, for he is good. His love endures forever."
Psalm 136:1

Allow the love of God and the Holy Spirit to flow through you to your family and friends and to those around you who may seem less desirable. Do not judge anyone today, just show and give the love of God freely to all.

DECEMBER 2, 2016
Friday
GOOD MORNING!

Last night worked out well. We went out shortly after midnight for coverage to Station 2. This morning I checked out the rig and reminded myself we need another portable oxygen tank. We have two spares right now but one of those is empty. The Battalion Chief just sent out the morning report and EMS drill is at its normal time. So off we go for the day. Good luck to me.

♦♦♦

WHAT A BUSY DAY. WE HAD drill and then numerous calls that kept us out until 8 p.m. Many of the people were quite sick and our last call was all the way out in Woodburn.

I wanted to tell you about a talk I had with my partner about our work here at the county. We were talking about my philosophy around being a probationary employee. I said, "I am not sure I know what probation really means because I will do what I'm told and will do a great job whether I'm a probie or not. Yet, they know me already and know I'm not going to just be pushed about and bossed around. What are they going to do? Fire me?" She laughed hard at that comment. Seriously, I do get ordered around by people with less experience and knowledge than I have but I let it go and just do what is right for my patient or the District.

In contrast, yesterday we worked with a man from Salem who was his normal (and expected) rude, jerky, and overbearing self. He *likes* to be rude and prides himself on how rude he can be not just to transport medics but also to his own people. Of course, he is allowed to continue with this bad behavior and has learned that if he is rude enough to everyone, no one will bother him or try to correct him because they don't want him to behave even worse than he already is. I find it amazing that people can be proud of how rude and obnoxious they are! I find it is a culture in many departments but it's not in my department. We have the five basic rules:

Rule #1 – Do what is right
Rule #2 – Do your best
Rule #3 – Treat others with dignity, understanding, & respect
Rule #4 – Leave the situation better than the way you found it
Rule #5 – Help other members to be successful

This all goes back to what I was saying last week. Remember the woman I took from the alcohol recovery center to the hospital? I showed her respect and treated her affliction with proper medical treatment. I showed compassion for her situation and didn't judge her. Do you remember? She thanked me for being kind to her and for treating her well. Then my Fire Chief was out with his work gloves hauling barrels around for the food drive. He was out in the cold along with the volunteers carrying and delivering barrels so we could feed the less fortunate. This rude man, this "public servant" for Salem, doesn't even care about his own people nor does he show respect for other medics, much less care about the less fortunate. He proves how "superior" he is by being so rude.

Please be like Fire Chief Terry Riley instead and give to others, respecting them and working hard for your team and for the community. Chief Riley is the real kind of hero. He doesn't just sit in his office, he is participating in his community to make it better and is busy serving the public. He doesn't just say it, he does it! Thank you Chief Riley.

Please go out and help someone in your community.

Well done good and faithful servant!…Come share in the joy of the Lord.

Matthew 25:23

The Lord is my strength and my shield; my heart trusts in him, and I am helped. My heart leaps for joy and I will give thanks to him in song.

Psalm 28:7

Good night and may you find joy and happiness in your faith.

December 7, 2016
Wednesday – Pearl Harbor Day Remembrance. 75 years ago.
What a day! When I arrived, we had to leave immediately for College Station 8 for a union meeting at 7:30 a.m. The meeting was interesting in and of itself since the Fire Chief was coming to talk to us. Then we had to complete a "fit test" for our SCBA breathing mask. I passed! So far I have had a fun and busy morning.

We had just returned to the station when we got a call for a fall. It was just up the street and when we arrived, the man was sitting in his chair. He had fallen at 2 a.m., though his real issue was a fever of 101.9⁰F and severe weakness. He was 104 years old and so we talked about Pearl Harbor and the British navy on the way to the hospital. When we got there, I gave my sheet with the patient's name and date of birth to the clerk. Most people just shove the computer at them and have the clerk try to find the name and birthdate on their own. I don't always accomplish this courtesy when I'm busy in the back of the medic with a sick or critical patient, but I try. The clerk smiled and said thank you. We then headed down to a room with the patient along with a nurse and med tech who came in to help move him from the stretcher to the bed. After giving the tech a courtesy briefing of what was going on with the patient, I went out to give a turnover report to the nurse.

I want you to know that the techs really appreciate a report. They are the ones who will continue treating the patient and it can be vital to know whether the patient fell, is coughing, what medications they've taken, or if they have pain somewhere. This protects the patient, protects the techs themselves, and helps them do their job. Very few medics tell the techs anything. I always try to get this report completed but in the rush to get to the next patient, I don't always accomplish my goal. This time, I was also able to give the nurse a verbal turnover report to supplement my notes and she appreciated that.

As I walked out of the hospital after delivering my patient, I felt so happy. Not only was I able to visit with the sick patient and hear his stories, I was able to take the time to be courteous to the clerk, tech, and nurse, and to make all their jobs easier. It feels amazing when all the pieces come together and I've done my job well. It's why I love my career—working on the street level with patients, techs, nurses, and physicians, and to have the opportunity to work together as a team showing respect and courtesy to everyone. I am fortunate even if others don't understand my love for the job and for other people. Thank you Salem Hospital Emergency Department for being great and awesome, too!

It's so important to provide great customer service to our customers. Who are our customers? Our customers are our patients, families and friends of the patients, the techs, nurses, and even the entire community as a whole. They are all our customers.

Our next call was for another fall. This time, the training officer responded as well since the call was in Brooks. He cancelled us as we pulled up to the house because it was a non-injury lift assist. I offered to come in anyway to help and he accepted. Once inside, we found a man had slipped to the ground and could not get up. He had then scooted from the bathroom to the front room so he could activate his medical alarm. The training officer and I helped him stand and got him back to his chair. I then picked up his medical alarm, smiled at him, and said, "Look, it has a watch band on it. You could probably wear this on your arm." His wife smiled and retorted that she has been trying to get him to wear it that way as well.

Back at the station, I had enough time to both start and finish my chart! Yeah! As I was beginning to get started on this star date log, the front door bell rang. Have I called it that before? This star date log is in honor of my son Victor 3 who has gone to Heaven before me. When I heard the bell, my partner was resting in her room so I jumped up to answer it and found this awesome and amazing woman at the front of the bay doors. She greeted me and said she has adopted this station and had freshly made homemade blueberry muffins to give us. I thanked her profusely and invited her into the bay to thank her again and get her name. She told me her son was in the military and he had recently been moved to the base in Washington so she needed someone to bake for in the area. How amazingly awesome and kind of her to make us goodies! She then told me that no one had asked her name all the other times she has left goodies for us at the station. Her name is Anne Bryant and

I'm going to write her a thank you card and have it ready the next time she stops by. With all the issues and problems life brings, these moments of thoughtfulness are precious and help our day so much. Thank you, Anne. Her son knows Corey and I will let him know that she stopped by the station.

A snowstorm is supposedly headed our way tonight and all day tomorrow. The prediction is for 2-4 inches of snow throughout the Salem area and for freezing rain in the evening. I'm actually looking forward to the next two days. I have long tights on, three layers of shirts, and I'll add a sweater later. I also brought my shoe spikes for walking in the snow.

I think that's it except to say I ate two blueberry muffins! YUM!

Good evening. We just got back from coverage and calls.

I was reading an article earlier today talking about how medics need to keep learning in order to be promoted to positions such as manager or Battalion Chief. One example was about a woman who had been in EMS for 20 years then quit her job as a supervisor to move into a higher management position. It made me think about my own career. I've worked hard to keep up with new developments in medicine—from 12 lead EKG interpretation and calling a STEMI, to IOs, computer charting, and the numerous advances in research, medicine, and treatment. I always have far more hours for recertification than required, sometimes I'm even over by a hundred. I've attended national conferences to get other points of view including the UCLA paramedic recertification classes to get fresh ideas from fresh faces. I've also attended two classes with the British Association of Immediate Care in England, am a member of BASICS, and a member of the Faculty of Prehospital Care of the Royal College of Surgeons of Edinburgh.

Though I have been a Shift Supervisor, the equivalent to Battalion Chief in that hierarchy, I always insisted on working in the field. While there, I would work two weeks in the field and then two weeks in the office. I enjoyed meeting the needs of the employees whenever I could but I actually prefer the field and helping patients directly. I sometimes think the people who head for the EMS office as quickly as possible are burned out by the field. Sometimes, they don't know how to lead or manage and weren't prepared for the position. I do not pretend to be a leader or a manager, I am a field medic and I believe myself to be a very good medic. From holding an older person's hand to patting their shoulders with reassuring touches, this is the best place for me *and* for my patients. I just love to be in the field. The next time you see a field medic on the street, often parked in a parking lot waiting for another call or at the store, thank them for their service and dedication. Don't just say you hope it's a slow day for them. Instead, say thank you for all their hard work taking care of the community.

Got a call!

DECEMBER 8, 2016
Thursday

IT'S BITTERLY COLD OUTSIDE THIS MORNING and we're supposed to get about two inches of snow with freezing rain in the afternoon. I've put four shirts on along with tights on my legs and will add a sweater later. So far, I've emptied all the garbage cans and will soon take the containers out to the curb.

Last night we had a call from the church on Pacific Highway in Brooks. A woman started slurring her speech and they called us. When we arrived, I talked to her and performed the Cincinnati stroke exam. She did fine except for the slurred speech. I then ordered an IV line and checked her blood sugar which was 59 mg/dL which is low for most people so we administered Dextrose and she was fine. The people called it a miracle. Well, it's a kind of miracle. Someone may have slurred speech or is unconscious and we wake them up and make them better by giving them sugar. It's amazing to watch. God gave people the intellect to figure this all out; it's a mediated miracle as my theology teacher Dr. O. Cope Budge would say.

I told the people at the church I'd been the Senior Minister Intern for Dr. George O. Wood in Costa Mesa and had attended SCC (Southern California College), now Vanguard University. They were happy we were the ones to help their friend. I love being in a job

where I can take care of someone and meet new people. Lord, please make today a great day, protect me, give me wisdom, and help me do well. Thank you Jesus.

The kitchen is now clean and the dishwasher is going as the snow falls outside. I'm going to drop off the spare set of spiked shoes in the medic for the frozen rain coming later today.

♦♦♦

It's been a busy day and I just finished my last chart. Our last call was for a woman with dementia who had abdominal pain. I think her gallbladder flared up with pain after the adult foster home staff where she lives gave her pizza to eat. She felt somewhat better when I moved her onto the stretcher but still wasn't comfortable so I gave her a dose of pain medication. When we arrived at the hospital, one of my favorite nurses looked at me skeptically when I told her the patient had abdominal pain since she looked just fine. I smiled and told the nurse I'd already given her 100 mcg of Fentanyl. "Oh, now I get it," she said. I was happy to have helped another patient and am glad to have the respect of the hospital staff. Being a positive presence goes a long way with both patients and medical professionals.

Earlier in the day, we'd responded to a lot of calls for falls, typical in this area for whenever it snows. There were falls on sidewalks, patios, roads, and driveways. To stay safe, I would advise people to get the paper later in the day, to not even attempt to walk on the snow and ice, and to just let the snow melt on its own.

I am hoping and praying I can make it through this year of probation.

December 11, 2016
Sunday

Good morning! I am working an extra shift on Medic 32 today as they needed extra staff and I took it plus two more shifts later this month.

We already had our first call for a woman with chest pain. She met us on the sidewalk and walked by herself to the ambulance. The pain has been going on for two days and is worse when her husband is around. I took her in for an evaluation and by the time we arrived at the hospital, she was calm and relaxed.

This last call is a perfect example of why I get so frustrated with Veterans Affairs. We had to transport a VA patient as he needed more colostomy bags and didn't know what else to do but call us to take him in to the hospital for more. Between the hospital bill and medic transport charge, it's probably costing $2,000- $3,000 just to get some help. When the man had called the VA, they told him it would take *six weeks* to get him more bags! You have got to be kidding me that some VA employee told him he would have to wait *six weeks* to get him something that he absolutely has to have! Amazon can deliver an item the next day! The people getting paychecks from the government have lost their good customer service attitude. They are there for only one reason: to do their job of providing good customer service and they have forgotten this fact. I have seen this in government a lot lately. People forget their purpose, are constantly unhappy, and then provide poor service. They prefer to pass on their unhappiness than to actually be thankful for the awesome government jobs they have and for the benefits they take for granted. It's so frustrating to see the VA not helping the very people who need their help. Let's call Amazon in to do their job instead.

I am thankful for this job at MCFD#1. Chuck, the charge nurse at the hospital, asked me earlier this morning if I was permanent and I answered yes. He said he saw me the other day, all smiles, and I told him I am lucky to come to the hospital and see my friends and colleagues. I am all smiles at the hospital; I am doing what I love to do.

♦♦♦

IT IS NOW 2:17 A.M. AND I just finished a chart. We responded to a call for a wonderful elderly lady who was having breathing problems and shortness of breath. We treated her and she was fine by the time we arrived at the hospital. I gave my report to a nurse I hadn't seen before and told her I hadn't started an IV because the patient didn't need one on the way. She said okay and I thanked her for understanding pre-hospital medicine to which she smiled and chuckled. I appreciated her understanding the humor in not starting an IV as some nurses get cranky when an IV is not started. This nurse understood not all patients need an IV. Thank you Marie for being so smart! Bless your heart.

All told, we've had 10 calls and 7 transports, many of which have been strange. One call was cancelled by dispatch right before we arrived. At midnight, we got a call to help the Woodburn police with an evaluation and before we arrived, that one was cancelled too. I am now going to take a nap for a while. Please get some rest yourself and say a prayer for all the firefighters and medics out there awake and working throughout the night.

DECEMBER 14, 2016
Wednesday
WE WERE HEADING TO A DRILL this afternoon when the calls started flooding in. Later on, after just arriving at the station to pick up some food, even more calls came in. It wasn't until two hours later when we were able to eat what we brought. Today, I'm working with Corey Kottek. He's a lot of fun to work with and he teaches me some bad (good) habits!

It's snowing again today and this time it will probably stick overnight. We've been busy as the snow has messed up the regular traffic flow. This evening, we had a call to take two boys to the hospital who tied their sled with a rope to their grandfather's truck and when he went to drive away, they went for a sleigh ride until the truck stopped and they plowed into the back of the vehicle. We then had more calls for several sick people. We are now back home at the station for a much needed rest.

While resting, I caught the last half of a Hallmark Christmas movie I couldn't understand the point of until the very end. The point they were trying to make is how our actions affect others for many generations to come. When a rock hits a lake, the ripples fan out and no one actually knows the effect the ripples have on the water. In the same way, when a person with love and compassion sets out to help, you never know the depth and length of the effect of that kindness. For example, by helping someone with their rent, heating bill, gasoline, or groceries, stress can be greatly lowered for both parents and children opening up room for more joy and happiness. Maybe the children get to eat a nutritious meal or have a warm house instead

Clear Lake Station, Station 6, home for tonight.

of simply noodles and sleeping outdoors. Years later, those children may bring you soup in your old age for they know the value of love and compassion for their neighbors. I hope I may continue to serve the community and the needy, to surprise those in need with help and understanding rather than judgment and loathing as so many others do each day. Lord, please help me help others and to anyone reading this, please go and help others as well. Remember that you can surprise people with love. Let's both love someone today and help them with their needs. Now go! Be an angel!

December 20, 2016
Tuesday

We were so busy yesterday (Monday) that I never had any time to sit down and write. It's now Tuesday and I'm grateful to have a bit of space to write and reflect.

We started off early yesterday morning with a call from up in the more rural area of the county. When we got close, we saw the fire truck parked on the side of the road. There was just too much ice for them to continue down the sloping access road so we gave them a ride in the medic. When the hill started going back up, though, we couldn't drive on the ice either so we walked up the rest of the way to the house where we found a 60 year old woman with schizophrenia in a group home. The report we'd received was that she had blue lips and couldn't keep her head up but I think she was sleeping as she looked fine when we saw her. I checked her blood pressure, pulse, and blood glucose and even took a stroll with her around the kitchen alongside her with her caregiver on one arm and myself on the other. She was full of smiles. I told her to have a beautiful day and she smiled so big and wonderful that the staff commented that they hadn't seen her smile so much in a long time. They said I was sweet. I was feeling silly and said my middle name was sweetness to which we all chuckled and they thanked us for coming out and checking on her.

Once I was alone with the Captain, I apologized for being so silly. The poor lady just sits all day long and this morning she got special attention and a walk around the kitchen. He said I have great bedside manner, that the patient was happy, and that I did a good job. Put a little love in your heart! The world will be a better place for you and me as the song says. Kindness should be our guide and I gave my patient all the love and kindness I had to give!

Now came the fun part: getting the medic out of there. My partner for the day was Corey, a firefighter-paramedic float, who was driving the medic. We tried pulling forward but couldn't make it out through the snow and ice so I jumped out to make sure he didn't slide off the road while Keith, the engineer of Engine 305, guided him out. After two more tries and a fast running start, we got the medic out of the long dirt driveway. Between the mud, snow, and sheet of ice, the driveway was a yucky mess but it was still very sweet to love on a person who doesn't get much happiness and fun.

This morning we responded to a call at 6:56 a.m. for a person who was experiencing severe shortness of breath. When we got there, the engine crew helped us get her into the ambulance where I started treating her with nebulized albuterol and oxygen. When I started to set up an IV, she told me she had bad veins and no one could get an IV on her. Well, she did have tiny veins but all I needed to give her was medication so a small needle would work just fine. I started a 22 gauge and she was surprised! My first attempt was successful and she received dexamethasone. By the time we got to Silverton Hospital, she was able to move good air in with every breath, no longer wheezing, and could now talk in sentences. Overall, a huge success.

The nurse I talked to at the hospital knew me and offered her condolences for the recent passing of my mom. She didn't know I was at MCFD#1. I told her after 35 years of working in Portland and Salem, I was happy to be working for Marion County. She gave me an early Christmas present by telling me I looked 40 so I told her I was the 63 year old probie. Hahahahaha!!! I also told her that last

Saturday was the 25th anniversary of my dad dying in the crash on Wilco Highway and again, she expressed her condolences.

I remember the accident so clearly. It was December 17, 1991 and I was watching Victor's basketball game. Though I had a fire radio with me, I had turned down the volume so I wouldn't bother anyone around me. During one of the timeouts, though, I heard Life Flight calling Mt. Angel Fire. I immediately left the gym to find a payphone and call my mother who listened to the emergency radio. She told me there was a very bad crash on the highway and since, at that time, we could respond directly to an incident, I decided to go out and help the crew.

After parking my Mustang by the Wilco Farmers plant, I walked up to the crash site and could see Life Flight, ambulances, and fire trucks on both sides of the crash, Silverton Fire on one side and Mt Angel Fire on the other. The highway was totally blocked.

My friend and colleague Larry Andres quickly came up to me to tell me it was my dad. In that nanosecond, my brain thought my dad was being bossy since he was the retired Fire Chief and often volunteered on the ambulance. "No," Larry said, "you don't understand."

Again, in that nanosecond my brain interpreted what I thought he said and so I replied, "Just put him on my elbow and he will listen to me. After all, I am the paramedic and he is the EMT."

"No," Larry insisted, "He is dead."

"Alright," I said, "Where is he?"

"Over there," he said.

I walked over to the body Larry had pointed to and lifted up the blanket. *No one* was telling me my dad was dead but me. Just as I was taught by John Moorhead, M.D., I looked at him from his feet to his head. "Just start at the feet and go up and you will learn what you want to know." Well, I did learn my

This is part of a billboard that Dad was on before he died. He was so proud. Victor 3 was very close to his grandpa.

dad was indeed dead, white as a ghost. His chest had taken out the steering wheel and he must have torn his aorta. All the blood was in his chest. I covered him back up.

The fire engine had a suitcase cell phone in it and I had to call my mom to tell her about Dad along with finding out where my son Paul was. When she picked up the phone, I asked, "Is Paul there?" "No," she replied. Now I was even more worried. Both my sons, Victor and Paul, were headed to Civil Air Patrol with their mom Lynell and there was no way to get a hold of them. I tried to clarify, "Lynell already picked up Paul?" "No, Paul is with your dad." Icy fear gripped my heart, "Oh my gosh! Don't let Lynell leave, I've got to go!"

I ran over to Dad's car and could see the car had been struck head on by another car that had left its lane and crossed over into my dad's. (This was later verified by witnesses.) With growing horror, I saw the engine of the huge new solid Chrysler New Yorker firmly lodged in the front seat! I ripped open the passenger door and started searching for Paul on the floor boards. No Paul to be found but I kept searching and thinking that in the chaos they missed finding him. A firefighter saw me looking and came up to tell me Paul had been found but was unconscious so he was taken to the hospital.

I remained calm, surprisingly calm. I walked over to my dad, knelt down next to him, and uncovered his head and chest. It was like I was suddenly in Heaven and was talking to his soul and spirit. My soul was talking to his soul and he was talking to me. It was and remains to be an indescribable experience. In those moments, I was covered by the ultimate peace of God.

Suddenly I felt an explosion inside! Someone had touched me and it broke the connection like a bomb had just gone off. I was knocked off the cliff and fell back to earth into the deep abyss of reality.

I rose to my feet and found a ride to the hospital where they had taken my small son. There, the on-call doctor told me Paul was fine but when I went in to look at him, I knew he was *not* fine. A three year old should be crying and moving around, not lying there limp.

The medical staff were pouring in normal saline into his body unnecessarily and had caused a bleed trying to put a Foley catheter in him. I told the doctor in no uncertain terms that my son was very ill. He disagreed with me and told me he was fine but I told that doctor he needed to stop infusing all that fluid immediately. He retorted back that Paul had a traumatic brain injury and so needed fluid but I knew he was wrong and the fluid overload all but killed Paul.

I ordered him to enter Paul into the trauma system and to then send him to Emmanuel Hospital in Portland. The doctor again told me Paul was fine and to not get so worried. I insisted, though, and won the debate. Paul was going to be sent to Emmanuel. The hospital ordered Life Flight which the dispatcher said had a 20 minute ETA but I knew the helicopter was on the ground at the crash site. It would be another two hours before they could fly to Portland, refuel, and get back down to the hospital to pick up Paul so I tried to intervene by asking that he go by ground instead. I lost that battle, though, and so I headed home to Mt. Angel to pick up the family and meet the helicopter in Portland. Even with all that extra driving, we still arrived in Portland by the roads before the helicopter ever got to Emmanuel with Paul.

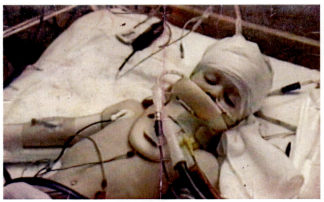

Paul on Christmas Day, December 25, 1991

Today, Paul is still alive. I saved his life that day back in 1991 by getting him to the right hospital where the pediatric neurosurgeon saved him there in the ICU. I am told that Dr. Marty Johnson's tie went flying one way and his coat the other when he saw the condition Paul was in. They immediately went into surgery where he drilled Paul's head to relieve the pressure from the bleed and all of the fluid overload. My son ended up with brain bleeds and was unconscious for two weeks. We spent the time playing Thomas the Train Engine videos for him for two solid weeks until he woke up hearing Thomas and seeing his doctor standing in front of him. He actually moved his head to look around Dr. Johnson! Everyone was so happy.

We were told that Paul would be mentally disabled for life. Today, he has a Bachelor's degree in Systems Engineering and a Masters in Civil Engineering from the University of Arizona. He is a Wildcat through and through! I am so proud of him.

We buried Dad while Paul was in Pediatric ICU, still near death and unconscious. This was particularly hard on Victor 3 as he so fiercely loved his grandpa and baby brother.

That whole time period reminds me of Isaiah:

Fire Chief Vic Hoffer and Victor Hoffer on
November 4, 1987

The children are exhausted and the people all give up
Yet those who have HOPE in the Lord will receive new strength;
They will fly like eagles,
They will run and finish the race,
They will walk and not fall down.

Isaiah 40:28-31

I was not flying or running, but somehow, I did not fall down. My heart is filled with so much I'd like to say about my dad, Victor 3, and Paul but, for now, suffice it to say that I love them all so very much. Now please go and hug your family, be kind to your neighbors, and give grace and understanding to others around you.

Learn to do right,
Seek justice,
Defend the oppressed,
Take up the cause of the fatherless,
Plead the case of the widow.

Isaiah1:17

This is what my dad, my Victor, and my brother John did their entire lives. I am trying my best. Pray for me that I have success.

December 22, 2016
Thursday
I am working a shift in return for the trade I made a couple of weeks ago and have spent the time in the computer room going through the new 2017 protocol. Though it's a new protocol for us here at MCFD#1, basically it's the Tri-County Protocol currently used in Portland. Having served for many years on the committee who wrote it, including serving as the Vice-Chair for one of those years, I'm pretty familiar with the protocol already.

The one protocol I wrote myself for the committee is the Aspirin protocol for chest pain. It's even noted in the original Washington County protocol that I'm the one who wrote it as it was the first of its kind in the state. I still have all the research I did somewhere at home and am proud to say it has stood the test of time.

With the new protocol in mind, I am putting together the medication list for what we need to add to the medical kits, which medications we need to remove, and which medications are staying. I am also putting together three papers for the BC.

I had a strange call with Keizer Fire today for a person with dementia who seemed extremely confused. Though it's normal for a dementia patient, we were told to take her in for "increased confusion." They told me at Keizer Fire that I am always smiling and ready to help. That was nice of them to say so.

There is no question that a smile is the best medicine for most everything. So please, go be pleasant and be happy and smile. Stop *trying* to be happy and just *be* happy.

December 23, 2016
Friday
I am at Station 1 on Medic 31 today. Coming straight from Medic 33, I brought all my stuff with me: turnouts, boots, helmet, and food as well.

Though I checked the medic and washed it first thing this morning, the medic is already dirty. It's been a busy day running calls. The first call was for an elderly lady with shortness of breath and very swollen feet, ankles, and lower legs. We had just returned from that call and I was thinking I would warm up my breakfast but we got another call.

The second call was for an 18 month old baby girl with a febrile seizure whom we took to the hospital. We hadn't even made it back to the station yet when the next call came through for a person having a syncopal episode at the grocery store. I've now just finished his chart and sent it on to the hospital.

Our most recent call was a "CPR call." That's a term our local dispatch team uses when a call comes into the 911 center and it sounds like CPR will be needed. We blasted out to that call as it was way out past the Pratum Station where we found a person who had already died. His body was already in the rigor mortis stage so there was nothing we could do but pronounce him dead and turn the scene over to the Sheriff. It's so sad for the family. Their dad has died. I know how that feels.

I would like to tell you about my brother John. He was in a crash on this day back in 1999 while driving to Tillamook, Oregon. Leslie Hoffer, his wife, called me to tell me of the accident and so I went to the hospital to spend the night there waiting with her along with helping and sitting with John and talking to him, though he was unconscious. He died the next day on December 24th, Christmas Eve, at Emmanuel Hospital, the same hospital my son Paul was at eight years before.

This is the one time I can ever recall using all three of my educational arts at once: theologian, paramedic, and lawyer. While sitting there with Leslie, we talked about God, medicine, and the law. I explained the medical jargon and read all the papers to her, including the donation papers, prayed with John, and just sat with him talking to him about life and thanked him for being so good to me.

Every day someone is having a difficult time with life, finances, relationships, jobs, school, or something

In Loving Memory

John Victor Hoffer
1945-1999

My brother John, died Christmas Eve day, December 24, 1999

else. How about we all show a little love, kindness, and courtesy today to someone. Actually, let's show it to everyone.

Remember kindness during this Christmas season and all year round.

And the multitudes were questioning John the Baptist asking what shall they do and he said to them: Let the man who has two coats share with him who has none; and let the woman who has food, share her food with others.

Luke 3:10-11

Paul stopped in to see me for a few minutes. He brought his girlfriend Amanda. I showed them the station and just as we began to chat, we got another call.

One of the calls we got today came in just before my partner was to get off work. We rushed to the call, then to the hospital, then back to the station and, amazingly, he still got off on time. The call had been for a person I had taken in four days ago for syncope. She is not having a problem with dizziness this time, though. She was experiencing pain from a previous injury. When I moved her, she held her arm up so it wouldn't flop and held onto her mobile phone as well. As always, I treated her with kindness and let her daughter ride in the back of the medic with us.

I have been working on the new protocols all day between calls but I'm now tired and ready to stop.

We had a head-on crash on Silverton Road at midnight where we had to cut off the door to rescue the patient out of the car. It was a very serious accident. We drove code 3 with a trauma entry to the hospital. Just as we cleared that call, we had another call to assist the police. A man weighing 325 pounds was intoxicated in the back of a police car and needed to be taken to the hospital.

DECEMBER 25, 2016
Sunday – Christmas Day

AFTER CELEBRATING CHRISTMAS WITH MY FAMILY last night, I started
my shift at 6:30 this morning and hadn't been in the station for even
20 minutes when we received the first of three calls and three coverages, one on top of another, and now another call has just come in.

♦♦♦

GOOD EVENING. IT'S NOW 7:17 P.M. and we are back home at the
station. Today we've had a total of five calls and four coverages.
One of the calls came in just as we were going to head to Station 2
for dinner with the other crews. We finally got to join them after
transporting the person to the hospital.

I wanted to say so much this morning about faith and life and
sadness, and somehow, overcoming sadness. That has all washed away
now. This time of year has always been a sad time for me. When I
was a child, I would go to the hospital for surgery the day after
Christmas. In those days, they made the parents leave at 6:00 p.m.
and children were left alone after that. I suppose that is why I find
peace in the solitude of being alone. I had many days and nights as
a child of being alone in the hospital and learned many things there
about life and a lot about death and suffering. I learned about the
suffering of humankind, how some of us are luckier than others, and
how others are luckier than us. I think it's best to find something
good in today in spite of the circumstances.

One of my most vivid recollections of that time in the hospital is
going in and out of consciousness after surgery when I was eight years
old. When I woke up, there was a smaller boy in my bed jumping
on me! He was playing and I would pass out again. Such are the ins
and outs of recovery from anesthesia. Anesthesia would make me so
sick back then. One time when I woke up, the mom of that little boy
and my mom were talking. As it turns out, she was from Monitor

Me and Paul. Christmas Day, Station 2. Sunday, December 25, 2016

which is a town close to our home in Mt. Angel. Her little boy had his head wrapped up in bandages and gauze just like mine and thus we both looked like astronauts with huge helmets on our heads. I eventually passed out again and don't remember anything else about that day. The next day, though, I was allowed up and about and so I went looking for the boy so I could play with and entertain him. I found my favorite nurse to ask about him and she told me he had died overnight and was gone.

While I was there at Good Samaritan Hospital recovering, I entertained many of the other children there. I would push kids around in wheelchairs until their moms would arrive during visiting hours or play board games with the kids who were confined to bed. I also loved working the dumbwaiter by pushing the call button until it came to our floor and then shoving open the door to yell that it had arrived. If I didn't open the door and hold it open, it would go back down before the nurse could come to pull out the children's medications from the pharmacy.

December 26, 2016
Monday

WE'VE BEEN RELATIVELY BUSY WITH A 5 a.m. call and then a car fire. The car fire was for a stolen GMC SUV which had since been abandoned and set ablaze.

December 31, 2016
Saturday

GOOD EVENING. WE'VE BEEN SO BUSY these last couple of days and I'm tired. I worked Friday at Station 2 and then today and tomorrow here at Clear Lake. There is so much I want to write yet I'm worn out from being so busy yesterday then handling drills and calls all this morning and afternoon.

I feel frozen in my mind. My brain says not to be sad yet my heart *is* sad. Dad died on December 17, 1991, John died on December 24, 1999, and my Victor 3 died on January 2, 2009. Right now, all I can do is remember that missed opportunity on New Year's Day to spend one more hour with my son Victor 3. I was trying to help my company by going up to Seattle to pick up a vehicle and then back home all in one day. Not knowing this, Victor 3 tried coming over to visit with me but when he saw my car was gone, he assumed his mom was gone as well and never tried going in to say hello—or what turned out to be the ultimate goodbye. My sadness this time of year is overwhelming. The loss of all three weighs heavy on my mind and heart while I'm trying to take care of so many other people during a long shift. I feel weak just trying to write and explain it all. This is where I pin my hope, hope I've made a difference and will continue to make a difference in my society for those still alive, that I've given something of value to humankind and have made life easier for someone else out there.

I am very sorry but I just can't talk right now. What do I say? Here I am at 63 years old trying to be a probationary member of Marion

County Fire District #1. My dad is gone. Though he has been gone for 25 years now, he is *still* gone and I need him here with me. He always took care of me. We ran calls together at Mt. Angel Fire. Victor 3, for some reason, wanted to be like me. He got his EMT license and we were going to work together at the ambulance company in Salem. If he were still alive, we would both be in Mt. Angel right now, volunteering together. I think he would have gone to law school as well and we could have had a practice together, a law practice where we actually charged clients and made money. He always gave away everything he had; we are alike in that way too. We both wanted to help the disenfranchised, the poor, and the underserved in our community. But they aren't the only ones who would have benefited by his presence. I still need him here too.

There are times to be sad. This is one. There are times to smile. This is one. That makes me confused. Faith and hope are all I have to hold onto, to keep me going sometimes.

This is what is on the back of Victor's prayer card.

SUCCESS

To laugh often and much;
to win the respect of intelligent people and
the affection of honest critics and
endure the betrayal of false friends;
to appreciate beauty, to find the best in others;
to leave the world a bit better;
whether by a healthy child,
a garden patch or a redeemed social condition
to know even one life has breathed easier because you have lived.
This is to have succeeded.

Ralph Waldo Emerson

These are two pictures of my boy as he grew up

January

January 1, 2017
Sunday – New Year's Day

Do you know of the Love Bridge in Paris? It's the Pont des Arts pedestrian bridge where couples used to place a lock on the railing of the bridge then click it shut, locking it forever. They would then throw the key into the Seine River never to be retrieved, the lock never to be released. In each of our lives, we all have people we love but sometimes we let that love go and release the other person who we initially meant to hold forever. It can be a close friend with whom we have a misunderstanding and never resolve the issue or a family member we keep arguing with. A husband and wife can slowly drift apart and while doing their own thing, never really care about the other again. People and love can be inconsistent, unreliable, and a creator of pain. Maybe today you could call someone you used to be friends with, used to like or love, used to care about, and reconcile those differences. At the very least, remind them they have a friend who cares about them and is available when they feel lost in the world.

I had a colleague who wanted to go to school to become a physician's assistant and so I helped him write the application letters. He was hard working and dedicated himself to other people. After a while, he left the company for a better paying job with better hours and I hadn't heard from him since then. We were both working and too busy to reach out to each other. He died on Monday. He died by his own hand and it's awful. Please check on your friends and family today. Stop reading this, put the book down, and check on them right now!

Our human love is so frail. We make mistakes. We say and do the wrong thing at the wrong time. We believe the wrong things and make the wrong things important in our lives. Whatever the causes or reasons, we hurt other people and we hurt ourselves. Somehow we should place love, kindness, and forgiveness at the top of the important list. Money, cars, and houses should become less important and friends, people, and doing what is right should be the priorities in our lives.

Thank God for his love. Psalm 106 says to "Give thanks to the Lord, for he is good; his love endures forever." Make peace *today* with people, your family, and friends, and thank God for his enduring and forever love. Run to Him and allow yourself to be held close and *feel* the love of God. Life is not easy, allow the Lord to help you and bring you comfort and then pass on that love, understanding, and forgiveness to your friends and family.

January 2, 2017
Monday

Today is the anniversary of when my son, Victor 3, died and I want to share with you my story about him and the events leading to his death.

We spent Christmas together and he gave me awesome presents. We seemed to see a lot of things the same way. We were so much alike. He had earned his EMT license and was proud and I was proud of him; we both wanted to serve the community. He coached soccer, was a Captain in the Civil Air Patrol, and a Captain in the Army.

Victor 3 had recently designed a website with our name on it. It was really a tribute to community service and his grandfather. When he shared it with me on Christmas, I thought it was awesome. He had Dad, me, and himself on the website, along with EMTs and other community servants. I told him, "Great!" But then I told him he should take a couple of things off the site as they were things I was sensitive about and didn't want posted for anyone to see. We disagreed about it and that ended up being the last time I talked with him.

I worked the next few days on shift and called Victor 3 but didn't get a hold of him. On the first of January, I was asked to go pick up a vehicle in Seattle. Always being the helper, I said yes. Victor 3 decided to come over that day to see his mom and dad. When he saw my car wasn't there, he didn't come in, thereby missing his mom. The

Paul and Victor 3

next day, January 2, 2009, he was driving his Toyota Spider, Charlotte, to Mount Angel to see me. I was returning from a funeral of a physician friend in Portland when I got a phone call that my son had been in a crash. Though he had been driving his four wheel drive for weeks due to the heavy big snow we had the month before, that day the weather was beautiful and sunny when he left so he took the sports car out for the drive.

While on the way there, Victor 3 went through a small hail storm. The storm was only a couple hundred yards long on Silverton Road and he slowed to 35 mph from 55 mph to be safe. Unfortunately, there was a hill and my guess is that he shifted down in the ice to get up the hill, slid sideways, and was struck by another car. Since he had suffered a serious head injury in the Army years before, he simply couldn't survive another impact like that and he died.

MCFD#1 actually took him to the hospital that day.

The person who called me told me Victor 3 was in a crash and that I had better get down there fast. It was an unusual request.

Charlotte, the car Victor 3 died in when he came home from the Army.

Normally a medic would have said, "Oh, he was in a crash and is fine, he just has a few bruises or a broken arm." (Or something like that.) I called the manager of the ambulance company in Salem and asked him to get to the hospital for me. I then called my wife but she didn't answer her phone. Lastly, I called the trauma hospital in Portland to see who the trauma doctor on duty was before hurrying to Salem. Talking again with the ambulance manager, he just kept saying I needed to get there fast. I knew what this meant: he was dead. I hoped I was wrong. In the meantime, I got a hold of Paul who was with his mother and they started toward the hospital.

When I arrived at the hospital, Doctor Nicole Vanderheyden MD, a wonderful trauma surgeon, met me at the door, brought me into the green room, and told me the news. "Your son is dead." I was calm and replied, "Okay, where is he?" Though she was there, ready to meet my needs and answer my questions, I had none. Between being a hospital chaplain and a paramedic, I knew all I wanted to do was see my son. I understood what she was saying. My precious son Victor was dead and there was nothing I could do to change that fact.

When Victor's mother and brother arrived, I told her the news and she screamed out, "NO!" I gently said, "Yes," and held her close. Paul was heartbroken and quiet. Paul wanted to go see his brother by himself so he went in before his mother and I went in to see him. In the room, one could feel the presence of angels waiting to take him away. There was a peace and a glow in the room even while there was deep sorrow in our hearts. I kissed my beloved son's forehead; he was warm and had no signs of injury. We then left with heavy hearts and the next day, I began to plan his funeral.

At the funeral home, so many people came to pay their respects. The military Honor Guard was present guarding his body while he laid there in his Civil Air Patrol uniform. So many friends came in

Victor 3 made these posters. Both images are of the truck Victor was a passenger in when he was severely injured in the Army. He was unconscious with a head injury for two weeks.

sobbing and overwrought with tears of sadness and loss. My chest was squeezed tight watching the overwhelming love people had for Victor 3. I was grief stricken myself yet still had to manage the events. I tried my best to stand tall for my Victor.

Governor Ted Kulongoski, Generals, Colonels, Majors, and more military personnel than I could have imagined came to his funeral. Fire Chiefs and firefighters, friends, neighbors, and many others came to the services. The Friends Church was packed and overflowing with people. My son received a full military burial and graveside service. An Honor Guard escorted his casket, taps were played, and he received a 21 gun salute.

Today, still, my heart is heavy with sorrow, torment, and sadness. All Victor 3 wanted to do was help his community and be like his grandpa and me.

JANUARY 7, 2017
Saturday

I AM AT MY NEW STATION at MCFD#1. This will be my new home for at least three months: Middle Grove Station, otherwise known as Station 2. This station is on two levels so we go up and down the stairs a lot to get to the living quarters and the medic. I'm excited about the stairs as they will help me get more exercise as well as the workout room here. Today is C shift, day 2. We were so busy yesterday, I didn't get a chance to sit down and write. Admittedly, I also haven't felt like writing about anything. As Victor 3 died around this time of year on January 2nd, I've been grieving all over again as I always do in January. Today I am feeling a bit better, though, so let's try to catch up on a few things and then get to work.

This year on January 2nd, I worked at the St. Paul Fire Department. It was okay. I was tired from the first 72 hours of working and then needing to pull another 24 hour shift. While there, I was assigned to teach an EMS drill that night on childbirth as well as giving a brief overview on Cannabinoid Hyperemesis Syndrome, a disease that was new to them. In between all that, I also went out on two fire calls.

Today I'm at Station 2 where we have Rescue 323 with us. These guys are hardworking and dedicated volunteers. They not only helped me chain up the medic, but my own car as well. It's snowing hard right now with freezing rain expected within the hour and then more snow. When I thanked them, they told me, "That's what we do, we take care of our own." I am part of us here at MCFD#1 and I am so thankful.

At times, it seems to me I can't do this job and then great people like the guys on R-323 look out for me and I start to think that maybe I *will* make it through probation. Thanks again R-323!

We took a call yesterday along with Silverton Fire for an accident on Silverton Road. There were multiple patients with five ambulances on the scene to transport them all. When we arrived, we received the most critical patient. I hope she survives; my heart has been so very heavy all night thinking about her. This girl is only 17 years old and had just said goodbye to her mom. Sitting in the front passenger seat, the car she was in pulled out in front of another vehicle traveling along the main highway and her side took the impact. Her mom heard the crash and ran down to find her daughter hurt and unconscious. The mom and I both fervently prayed that God would bring all my skills and knowledge to my mind to be there for me as I treated her daughter's traumatic brain injury. I understand the girl was flown to a trauma hospital from Salem but I don't know what happened after that.

I am going to take a moment now to eat while I can and then be ready for the gigantic amount of calls we're soon going to have because of all the snow and ice on the roads. Please love your family. Look out for the needy. Give to the poor.

I have a CALL. Oh my goodness. I literally just finished writing the above paragraph when we got a call.

♦♦♦

It's snowing like crazy outside. There are a lot of cars out there—they should just stay at home and be safe. At the intersection of Silverton Road and Cordon, a car was turning onto Silverton Road and slid on the snowy ice. Luckily, no one was hit. We went around the car as it was parked by then and the driver, a teenage girl, was busy collecting herself. She waved at us with such a precious smile as if to say, "Wow! Wasn't I lucky!" It was cute.

I'm going to try again to grab something to eat before we go out to another call. Show love and kindness.

Good morning. It's Sunday morning at 2:24 a.m. and I've just finished a trauma chart and sent it along to the hospital. We responded to a call for a person who was stabbed three times in the chest. I started a 16 gauge IV line, applied bandages, and applied pressure to the wounds. We had a six minute on scene time and did all our procedures while traveling to the hospital.

Good night. Believe, have faith, and do your best.

January 8, 2017
Sunday

I'm just finishing up my shift. We had two calls after 5:00 a.m. and now it's 9 a.m. and I've finished my charts. Soon I will be driving home in the ice and snow myself. I do this because I love to do it even when I am tired. Just keep smiling.

The hospital staff are tired too. Peter was there this morning and took my report. He's extraordinarily smart, a great manager and nurse, and he works very hard to support his staff there at Salem Hospital Emergency Department (SHED). Smile today.

JANUARY 12, 2017
Thursday

I'M AT STATION 2 THIS MORNING, the Middle Grove Station, on Medic 32. I've already checked the medic off and found we need lots of supplies. Frankly, it was kind of a mess. It's ready to go now, though, and if it warms up enough, I will wash it as well. It's fairly dirty from all the days with freezing temperatures and no washing.

For some reason, I've been struggling with life lately. Nearly every day I am working somewhere. I was here on both Thursday and Friday, at the OCC on Saturday, and then Sunday at St. Paul Fire. This time of year, of course, I really miss my dad and Victor 3. It's probably a bit harder for me this year as the snow storm we've been having has been compared to the snow storm that killed Victor 3 in 2009.

I've been listening to a song lately that originated from a 1936 movie by Charles Chaplin. Even today, he continues to have a lasting impact on people. You should look up the final scene of the movie, *Modern Times.* I've been listening to the Glee rendition; they use pain instead of fear and that works better for me. Here are the words Turner and Parsons wrote:

SMILE
Music by Charles Chaplin, Lyrics by John Turner
and Geoffrey Parsons

Smile, though your heart is aching
Smile, even though it's breaking
When there are clouds in the sky you'll get by
If you smile through your fear (pain) and sorrow
Smile and maybe tomorrow
You'll see the sun come shining through for you
Light up your face with gladness
Hide every trace of sadness
Although a tear may be ever so near

That's the time you must keep on trying
Smile what's the use of crying
You'll find that life is still worthwhile
If you'll just
Smile

I'm very concerned about the girl I took care of last week in the snowstorm. I stopped by her church yesterday to see if I could find out anything about her condition. There was no one there at the Apostolic Christian Church when I stopped by but I still do believe in miracles. One of my professors at Vanguard University (aka SCC), Dr. O. Cope Budge, taught me there were two kinds of miracles: one miracle is immediate and the other is mediated. Mediated miracles happen through people over time. God gave each of us the knowledge and skills to help each other. Doctors, nurses, and paramedics are just some of the miracle workers among many others. Researchers who find new cures are also creators of miracles. Each of us heal and save lives in our own way. As a paramedic, sometimes I wonder how I had the ability to do something. I think, "How did I think of that?" or "Wow, did I just use that skill in that way?" So I *do* believe in people making miracles by the grace of God who gives us all knowledge and skills.

Victor 3 with that great smile of his (and Charlotte)

Every day, there are EMTs, paramedics, firefighters, nurses, doctors, and many other people around the world saving lives. Just 100 years ago, far more people died from the same conditions people can now live through. Somehow, I like this more than being a lawyer or pastor or just about anything else I can think of. Maybe it's because I *do* surprise myself and I *do* believe I need God to be with me to care for and understand the people I take care of.

Believe in yourself and ask God to help you through your day. Bless someone by thanking them for being there and doing their job. Wherever you may be today, appreciate someone. Thank the grocery clerk for being there or the gas station attendant (in Oregon) for being so attentive, or the restaurant waiter for serving. Remember, those people are working for a living and they have a lot of people throughout the day who are rude to them. So how about you try being extra polite and appreciative, even if the line is long or the service is slow. Often, those things are a sign of poor management. It's not the fault of the person at the counter. Just appreciate them. Thank them. And thank you for doing that today and every day.

9:45 P.M.

I JUST CAME BACK FROM THE hospital. It is, of course, very busy, overworked, and understaffed. With all the snow and ice, I think everyone is tired both physically and mentally. A nurse asked me how I was doing and I replied that I was peachy like a peach. She chuckled and said, "Really!" Quickly, I related to her that over this time period in previous years I had lost my dad, brother, and my son all to traffic crashes and then lost my mom last year the day before Mother's Day. I asked her, "What choice do I have but to smile and be positive?" She hadn't heard of the "Smile" song. I truly and honestly do feel sad at times but I try so very hard to hold it under my skin in public. I don't know if she truly understood. It's hard to understand pain and suffering if you've never really suffered or lost someone close to you.

What I'm trying to do with this silly "star date log" is to help you through your own rough times. If you like any of the scriptures, quotes, or any of my ramblings, I hope you've found some happiness in them. I want us to share our faith, to hope in God, and to know His love for us in the middle of our suffering and despair. Call me if you like but, for now, good night. Dream happy dreams and have great dreams of your future.

Remember, you can never have too much *HAPPY!*

JANUARY 13, 2017
Friday the 13ᵗʰ and a Full Moon

WHAT A LONG DAY WE'VE HAD at MCFD#1 today! I got up and was in uniform before 7:00 a.m. when I checked the medic. We're low on oxygen but we'll go get some later today. After we returned from a call, we had drill until noon but halfway through, we responded to another call for an auto vs. bicycle crash on Lancaster Drive. When we arrived, an injured man was lying on the road. While my partner treated him, I drove them to the hospital with red lights and sirens. On the way back from the hospital, we stopped by a store to buy two dozen doughnuts for the crew back at the station, one of which I got to enjoy before going on another call.

The call we responded to was for a very sick lady with multiple medical problems. On the way to the hospital, I gave her some Fentanyl and Zofran to help her feel better. Once we arrived, I noticed all the staff seem stressed out. Being a hospital emergency department, it's a busy place with a lot of patients but the looks on the staff's faces were even more tense than usual. I keep trying to put on my smile for them, even when I, too, feel the stress of work and life. (Have I told you how amazing the staff is at Salem Emergency? They are!)

The call after that was for a hysterical man with shortness of breath. In addition to my partner and I, we also had James from Engine 305 assisting with the call. It was nice to have his help. As it was my partner's patient again, I drove to the hospital with sirens blaring. Heading down Lancaster to Portland Road, I slowed down at an intersection with a stop sign but no light to make sure we were clear to proceed. I cleared the left but when I looked to the right, there was a large white van whipping down the road and not stopping. The driver just kept driving toward the medic and didn't yield at all. I am so glad I slowed down to look, otherwise we would have been hit by that van as even with red lights flashing and sirens sounding, that van still just flew on by.

We were busy like that for most of the night and then this morning we had another strange call. This one came in at 6:00 a.m. for a young woman who became sick when she ate some cake at 4:30 a.m. The story she told us was she had gone to a party and then had cake of unknown origin at an after party. My guess is that the cake she ate was laced with marijuana Delta-9 THC and she was feeling the effects of the psychoactive ingredient including her racing heart and hyperventilation.

All in all, it was a long tour of duty. May I just tell you how difficult it is to smile when the day's difficulties have come upon us like a snowstorm? It's as if we're facing into blinding snow hitting us in the face and freezing our hands. At those times, it's hard to remember the promises of God, to see and believe when the snow is pounding against us and the wind is pushing us backwards. We try and step forward but are just blown back again and again.

I have been working 80 plus hours every week for a while now and I am truly mentally and physically exhausted. With all the effort I've been putting in, I'm feeling underappreciated and undervalued. Do you feel like your family, boss, and friends don't understand you or don't respect the value you bring to your family, job, and community? I am choosing to smile, how about you? Shall we smile in the face of the storm? Let's try. Let's believe and have faith, remembering that God's love endures forever. Even when we don't feel it, God's love is still there for us. I am going to smile and try to feel the love of God today. Maybe when all things come together, we'll find warm shelter in God. Through tough and inexplicable times, "we know that in all things God works for the good of those who love him." (Romans 8:28) I know you love God and that our suffering will be understood and taken away by His love. Smile big and long and let God give you the warmth of the day. (And pray for me.)

January 14, 2017
Saturday

WELCOME TO MY NON-PROBIE JOB. I am at the Oregon Convention Center today working medical standby for a cheerleading competition. I enjoy coming up here and helping solve problems for people. I've already handed out Tylenol, Advil, ear plugs, and ice packs. I'm in my room mostly so the kids can find me if they need me. One little girl, probably four years old, needed ear plugs because it was too loud for her in the hall while she watched her sister compete. Then an older competitor came in with a sore shoulder to whom I gave an ice pack. She was from the Salem team so I talked with her and her mother before sharing with them some Tinker Bell dust and stickers. They both had beautiful smiles on their faces when they waved goodbye to me. You can never have too much happy *or* Tinker Bell dust. I asked them to drive home safely.

I think a lot of people don't understand me. Do you remember Ruth from the Bible? She was an immigrant from Moab who needed help. Just as Boaz did, I try my best to show kindness to such as these. Let's all give to others in need, show charity, and be kind to everyone.

♦♦♦

A GIRL IN CHEER JUST CAME to my door for a bottle of water! Though water isn't commonly stocked in the medical room, I had a sealed bottle of water in my bag which I gave to her. I asked her if she needed some money, too, and she said no. I don't know where her coach or team are or why she is not being looked out for by someone. Finally,

I had a call just a minute before I was released for the day. No one could find or contact the EMT the promoters had hired to be on site so I took care of the injury. It's so frustrating. The company they use for EMTs doesn't send experienced people to any of these events; they are usually inexperienced and hired at the lowest cost. I know because I used to work for them. When I ran the program, it was excellent and even received an award of excellence from the Health Division but not anymore. I'm so happy and thankful to now be working for MCFD#1 and the OCC.

January 15, 2017
Sunday – St. Paul Fire

I NEED TO TELL YOU THAT I struggle with not knowing whether I have made a difference in the world or in my community. There is so much more for me to do for humankind but I'm just not sure how or where or when. I believe that part of the answer is *now* but I don't know the how or the where. If you are actually reading this, it means it was published in some form to be read. If you are feeling that you need to do more let me know and maybe I can help you find your answer. Most likely, your family and friends will tell you that you have done so much; please believe them. For today, let's believe, have faith, and hope together. Let's show love and kindness and give help to the poor, the disenfranchised, and the neglected.

The real story of this book is to bring hope to you. If I have failed, I apologize. For now, I continue to believe we must be kind. We must be kind every day, to everyone, and all the time. In *The Land of Oz* books by L. Frank Baum, King Rinkitink is described in this way: "His heart is kind and gentle and that is far better than being wise."

Be kind and compassionate to one another.

Ephesians 4:32

JANUARY 28, 2017
Saturday

GOOD MORNING. WHAT A WEEK I'VE had this week! My tour at MCFD#1 Tuesday and Wednesday was so busy that I didn't have a moment to sit down and talk with you.

We started off right away in the morning with EMS drills but before we could even get halfway through, we got our first call. After that, the calls wouldn't stop and we didn't finish until around ten in the evening then a few more calls came in at 1, 3 and 5 in the morning. The second day we started right at 7:00 a.m. after being up all night to cover the calls for Medic 31 as well as our own so they could run drills. When we finished running their calls, we went to the drill ground as well to drill until noon before running more calls. Those calls didn't stop until midnight. The next morning, we got ready for the Mt. Angel Fire public education fire station visit. This is by far my favorite thing to do for the community. On Tuesday, I was in charge of five and six year olds and on Thursday, I had three and four year olds from a local preschool. I always teach them to stop, drop,

Playing with the kids is a lot of fun for me!

and roll if they are ever on fire. As if it's a game, we run and then we stop, drop, and roll. I even do it along with them which the parents find amusing. We also have the kids put the gear on the firefighters so they won't be scared of them before we give them a tour of the fire trucks and then we have fun spraying water.

Right now, I'm here at Station 2, Middle Grove, for half a shift. It was going to be the complete shift but it was changed to only 11 hours. I'm so happy to go home and rest after this as I work tomorrow in Portland at the Expo Center.

Today I want to ask you to do me a favor: go be nice to someone. Please. Yesterday I saw Darrell at the Roth's in Silverton. He is such a joyful person and I really appreciate him just for being himself but also for coming to my mom's funeral. He and his wife used to go on the Elks' bus trips together and they formed a friendship with my mother. Then at the checkout stand, I saw the assistant manager, Barb, and chatted with her. I reminded her that her dad and I were the same age and went to school together. Barb said I didn't look like I was in my 60s and I laughed and told her that I appreciated people who told me I was younger looking than my real age. Some days, like today, I do feel old and tired but it makes me smile when I'm told I'm young-looking. I find it funny.

Today, though, I do feel old. I was on rescue duty in Mt. Angel last night and responded to a call at 2 a.m. for an unconscious critically injured person with a traumatic head injury. Medic 23 was already on the scene so while I hopped into the ambulance to set up IVs, the Medic 23 crew worked on loading the patient.

When they got her into the ambulance, she wasn't breathing so we needed to put a tube into her trachea to breathe for her. They were going to put in a King airway but I asked if I could have a try before they did. I looked in, suctioned her airway, and, fortunately, got the tube in place with the first attempt. It was difficult and took a team effort for success. We then went code 3 to Salem with a trauma and started IVs to give her medication. I later found out the patient survived and is fine! The trauma doctor told the patient's mother she would have died if we hadn't gotten the endotracheal tube into her trachea and were able to breathe for her on the way to the hospital.

Life is so precious and someone you love can be taken away from you in a heartbeat. So first, let's get home safely every day. Next, go hug your family and friends and tell them how much you appreciate them. Finally, let's help someone in need, big need or little need, it doesn't matter. Just find someone who may be under the radar, so to speak, and needs just a little help from you today.

Make sure you have no bias or prejudice against other people but treat everyone with courtesy and respect. Don't be the judge but be the kind-hearted person who accepts, understands, and helps all of humankind. Today, smile and show kindness to all people. Remember, in the end, whatever you did for one of the least of our brothers and sisters in the world you did it to and for God. (Matthew 25:40)

When I work a shift and don't have time to write things down, I feel like the thoughts are lost forever, never to return. One thing I do want to tell you about last week is that Mt. Angel Fire recognized the team of people who saved a 37 year old. The man had died but we brought him back to life. At the annual banquet we held last Saturday, he was there in attendance. I can't tell you how much it meant to me to see him walking around enjoying life. That is now two saves for Mt. Angel Fire over the last three years. I heard at the public education day that the other person was out snowboarding over the weekend. How exciting!

For myself, I was blessed, shocked, and humbled when I received the EMT/Paramedic of the Year Award and a Chief's Award. The EMT Award is voted on by the firefighters, my colleagues, and they think enough of me to award me for my efforts when so much of what we do is a team effort. Then the Chief presented me with his award. I was shocked and humbled all over again and am so thankful to my colleagues and friends for their kindness.

After the banquet, we got a call to help someone experiencing shortness of breath. When we arrived, Silverton Fire was already there as they were covering our station during the banquet and hadn't gone home yet. They told us the woman had gone into respiratory arrest and then cardiac arrest from a new trach which was plugged up. I removed the trach and put in an endotracheal tube so we could start breathing for her. Josh and Dale started CPR and the Medic crew attached the monitor while I pushed epinephrine. After four minutes into all this happening, her pulse was back and she started breathing on her own again. After having just celebrated a second save in the district, we now had a third. It was excellent teamwork.

Go out now and be kind and thankful.

January 31, 2017
Tuesday

It's been a busy couple of days for me on Medic 32 where I've had no time to sit down and talk to you. We had drill, coverage, and calls, in addition to me working on a $4,000 order for supplies and medications which took me several hours to create.

We responded to a lot of calls yesterday. One call that particularly stands out to me was for a 25 year old woman who cut her arm with a knife. By the time we arrived, the bleeding had stopped so I bandaged her arm and took her in to the hospital to have it stitched up. She didn't seem to want to hurt herself, she just wanted help from someone. She told me she's run out of her medications and knew she needed help. She also said she's on Medicare and Medicaid so I don't know why she doesn't have any more meds. Her ex-boyfriend is now in prison and she and her new boyfriend (she's living in an RV next to his house) had argued before he headed out to work. The hospital physician, I noted, was very kind to her and it sounded like he'll help her get settled. Of course, my worry is that she's being taken advantage of by these men since she must be getting money every month. My guess is they're taking the money away from her and holding her captive, at least mentally. It's a very sad situation for a 25 year old woman.

Today we've already run several calls and just got back from one in Silverton. I want to do the best job I can here at MCFD#1. My partner for the day, Matt, is smart and has been helping me with computer work in between calls. I deeply appreciate what a good medic he is and how hard he works.

I just heard back from the hospital that the 17 year old girl we took care of the other week in Mt. Angel is improving greatly! I'm so happy and grateful I could be a part of helping her live. I simply cannot do this job without the grace of God being with me as I make critical choices at the scene of an accident or in the transport on the way to the hospital. With a humble and thankful heart, I will be able to help even more people who need a kind hand. My strength to do this work comes from God and when I'm with my colleagues and patients, I must remember to be utterly humble and gentle, to be patient, showing love and respect to all people. (Ephesians 4:2) Thank you to the angels and saints who look out for me as well. Thanks Dad and Victor 3. I believe they are here too.

FEBRUARY

FEBRUARY 9, 2017
Thursday

WHAT A WEEK I'VE HAD! SUNDAY and Monday were both incredibly busy days. I then worked in St. Paul on Tuesday. Thank goodness I had yesterday off because by the time I got to Wednesday, I was so tired both mentally and physically that I slept the whole day. Today I feel a sore throat coming on.

Sunday was Super Bowl Sunday and we had calls starting at 6:45 in the morning that went straight through, call after call, until 3:30 the next morning, including four during the game and five more afterwards. Needless to say, we only caught a few minutes of play ourselves but that's normal for us. In fact, I haven't seen a complete Super Bowl game in many years. On Monday, I was up and dressed by 7:00 a.m. for drill, more calls, and ordering needed medications and supplies.

During one of our trips to the hospital, I talked with a clerk I've known for many years. She looked overworked and a little sad so I tried pulling up the "Smile" song to cheer her up but we couldn't get any sound. I shared how I listen to it every day so she wrote the title down and will listen to it later. She commented to me that I always smile and she needed one of those today. I then shared with her that when Victor 3 died in the crash and my heart was so heavy with loss and pain, I wouldn't have been able to listen to it at that time. Today, I still have the pain and his death still stings but I do my best to share my funny smile with everyone and especially to those who work at the hospital. The staff there work so hard taking care of people that they can easily become worn out.

Today when you go out shopping, keep your head up and your heart full of love and smile at everyone who looks your way. So many people are too busy looking down, avoiding people, and focusing on the negative, and it's often because they are too busy, angry, hurt, or sad. Please smile at everyone and let your aura be happy and bright.

We are all in this together. We are a team. Let's all spread smiles and love while we give to those in need. Thinking of the marches that have gone on lately, I wish those same people each gave $10 to a mission, a homeless shelter, or a food bank. March all you like, express disdain for others' opinions, but give $10 today to the poor, the needy, and the disenfranchised. *That* is putting your money where your mouth is. In the Bible, James reminds us to do more than to simply go to church on Sunday and listen to a sermon. He encourages, if not admonishes, us to all go out and take care of people. Please find someone to help today. Smile at someone. Bless someone's life with the love of God shining through you today. Pray for me too!

FEBRUARY 12, 2017
Sunday
WE'VE BEEN INCREDIBLY BUSY AND WERE up all day and night...

FEBRUARY 18, 2017
Saturday
SO VERY SICK. VOMITING UP BLACK blood, I was sent home by the Chief.

FEBRUARY 24, 2017
Friday
VERY BUSY AND UP CONSTANTLY AT NIGHT.

FEBRUARY 25, 2017
Saturday
GOOD MORNING! WHAT A BUSY LAST two weeks!

"There but by the grace of God go I." This phrase is credited to John Bradford (circa 1510-1555), an evangelical preacher and martyr. We go to many places with people who are poor, drug addicted, and mentally ill. Sometimes our compassion quotient is stretched thin and it's at those times when I remind myself of this phrase. We had an elderly patient yesterday who was a pleasant person to deal with but who is experiencing difficult circumstances. Currently living at the Union Gospel Mission, he became ill and took a bus to the doctor's office. He was so sick, though, that they called us to come take him to the hospital. He wants to be healthy, he doesn't want to die. Even though he lives in a shelter with hundreds of other people, he has no one. What a sad thing. He is trying but has no family who love him. Yes, there may be reasons from the past why his family has abandoned him, I am not here to judge. But maybe forgiveness and love could prevail for him. The real point is that it could be you or me in this position. There but by the grace of God go I…

This is why we need to be so kind to other people. We should show understanding and help them whenever we can. Just be compassionate.

We also had a call for a man with a heroin addiction. He tried to shoplift four 50¢ snack pies from a grocery store and was tackled and handcuffed by a 300 pound man. Having sustained a ribcage injury, they called us to the scene. I asked the store owners if they were going to ask the police to prosecute the man for the pies and the indignant response was yes. Between the medic ride, the hospital evaluation, the fire engine response, and the police response, it probably cost over $5,000 to respond to a $2 theft. Society needs to figure out how to treat the addicted, not laugh at them and do them harm. There but by the grace of God go I…

I don't usually give money to people on street corners. Having taken care of many of them, I know they spend that money on drugs and alcohol. Every newspaper I've ever read has run at least one article on the gangs of people who control intersections and look for money for more drugs. I am sure you know and understand the people I am talking about when you look to help someone. Please do help people, though, and, on occasion, you may help the person who is a manipulator or professional taker. Just let it go and keep helping those in real need. Remember, there but by the grace of God go I…

The first call we received on the 22nd was for a man who had been having chest pain since 3 a.m. While giving him aspirin and getting ready to take him to the hospital, his heart stopped, he stopped breathing, and he died. We started CPR, shocked him once, and I started an IO (intraosseous—a needle in the leg bone) to give him medications. When I flushed the line, he said, "Ouch!" At that, we stopped CPR and he woke up and started breathing again. We then immediately took off to the hospital where they found he had a 100% occlusion of a coronary artery. They treated it by ballooning the artery and he will go home in a few days. We saved his life. He was dead. He would not have survived if we had not been there. A life saved.

For all the people who treat you poorly, remember that you are important. To be a millionaire is not the end all of success. Having compassion and helping others is real success.

Do you remember that 17 year old girl we treated back in January after a car accident on Silverton Road? It was the one where her mother heard the crash just after her daughter had left her house, ran to the cars, and found her daughter unconscious and bleeding. On our way to the hospital with lights and sirens blaring, I entered her into the trauma system and began my magic. I *always* ask God for help on calls like this. I pray that all my knowledge, experience, and skill will be there for me to help me save a life. In case Dad and Victor 3 can hear me, I ask for their help too. This girl was unresponsive, then would wake up for a few moments and vomit before becoming unconscious again. I did all the things paramedics do on our way to the hospital.

Knowing her mom was from the Apostolic Church just up the road from the crash, I talked with her for a moment in the ER while her daughter went for a CT scan so I could tell her my story of Charles Wesley and his experience of praying in the calm and trusting in God during the storm. Then I told her I would send my Legion of Angels from God to be with her daughter and who would shelter her with God's love and help the surgeons. She smiled and I continued to pray and hope as I left to run more calls throughout the day. Later on during another call, I saw the physician who treated the girl and he told me things looked very grave indeed and that death was at hand. My heart was so sad and all I could think to do was to pray and remind my Legion of Angels to be taking good care of her.

Just this week I found a note in my box at Mount Angel from the girl's mom telling me how well her daughter is doing.

Most people don't understand why I do what I do, especially at this older age. They don't understand why I would rather be a probie than be in an office bossing people around. Reading this, do you understand?

Lori is nearing a full recovery—nothing short of miraculous by all Dr.s remarks. She had fractured skull and orbital fracture and brain bleed. We were @ OHSU 4 days and have seen and felt how God can work. Thank you for your "help" in commanding that legion of angels!!

Lori Walter
Silverton rd
+ 81st Ave
1/6/17

God's Mercy
Evident

Victor Hoffer—
Thank you and God bless you for your loving kindness to me in the Salem ER. Your words of encouragement meant so much to me and your faith led me to witness likewise to others.
In Him—Megan Walter

MARCH

MARCH 7, 2017
Tuesday

HAPPY ANNIVERSARY TO ME! I WAS hired as a temporary employee at MCFD#1 one year ago today.

(My civil service hire date is September 12, 2016.)

I AM FEELING DISAPPOINTED IN MYSELF today. It's now very late and I still have several more charts to complete. I do know I'm luckier than the patients I've taken care of today yet I feel so off and I'm wishing I could pick myself up.

MARCH 8, 2017
Wednesday

GOOD MORNING. IT'S 4:57 IN THE morning and I just finished a chart and sent it to the hospital.

Today if you are reading this, please pray for me along with all medics and firefighters.

We had a lot of calls yesterday and each person was in the middle of awful circumstances. I am lucky in so many ways. In between the calls, I worked on ordering supplies and figuring out the budget for the coming year. I'll present my budget proposal today and am happy to say it's only a 2.34% increase over last year's budget.

What is most important to me today is people. So many people are in such sad circumstances. Between ill health and poverty, they don't know how to overcome their situation. Of course, some require financial help to better their lives, the help that comes from you. I know this is repetitive, but we *must* act as a community and help each other. I believe we should first make the real difference at home through helping our neighbors and those across town. Even just $5-20 to the little girl or boy down the street who has nothing goes much further than the money that so often sifts through so many executives. It's okay to help globally, yet helping your local community and neighbors is also needed and the results can be quickly seen.

MARCH 10, 2017
Friday

I WAS WATCHING THE TELEVISION SHOW, *NCIS,* yesterday and Gibbs was talking to Doctor Mallard about his health and, ultimately, the Director, Jenni's, health. Doctor Mallard said Gibbs was healthy for a person of his age. That's a good way to look at my health too. Here at MCFD#1, I have a vitamin box I bring in for every tour. Though different people like to rib me about it, exercising is part of my health routine so I can keep up with everyone else at the District. During my last tour, I worked out lifting weights in the weight room, not like the younger guys, of course, but I work at it. While talking with some of my friends from Salem Fire, they asked me how I like it here. I told them it was great, that everyone is so good to me, they respect me, my knowledge, and all the experience I've gained over the last 37 years. The guys at Salem Fire are really good to me whenever we have a call together. I'll walk in and ask, "How can we help?" and we work together to make someone's life better. I'm in good health and I want to stay that way so I can continue to care for others at MCFD, St. Paul Fire, the Convention Center, and Mt. Angel Fire.

I like to think of myself as the Gibbs of EMS. I've trained so many people here that I feel like they are my EMS children. I enjoy seeing these new medics become successful. One of them, Tim Verdun, taught an awesome training on humeral intraosseous infusion insertion the other day. Both clear and informative, he taught me how to do a procedure which is new to me. I trained him many years ago and so I told him the student had become the master. He is very professional and a great success. I am so proud.

The best things for me here at MCFD #1 are seeing my colleagues be successful, saving lives, and on occasion, receiving a thank you for a job well done. The other thing that makes me feel great is to receive a compliment myself. A "good job" from the Chief, another firefighter or medic, a patient, or a friend always makes a day better. Yesterday, Mr. Piatz paid me an awesome compliment. I was at Roth's Market, the best hometown market anywhere, when he came up behind me in line. Before I could remind him he was once my teacher and that I am now saving lives because of his great training as a teacher and coach while I was in grade school, he looked over to the checkout clerk I had been visiting with and said, "He is one of mine." Wow! I am one of his boys! He not only taught me the curriculum, but he also taught me how to throw a baseball and how to persevere through challenges.

When I was in grade school, there was a day at lunch recess when we were playing softball. Though I had no athletic talent, I was pitching when I ran to first base to catch the ball and dropped it in front of me. I picked it up and moped back to the pitching mound where Mr. Piatz told me to let it go and keep going. Perseverance. Yes, dropping the ball was a totally insignificant thing but at that moment, I was so embarrassed at my lack of athletic ability. Many others helped me learn this skill as well: Dr. Willard Rowland who oversaw the numerous surgeries I had as a child, Rev. Dr. O. Cope Budge, Rev. Dr. Russell Spittler, and Rev. Dr. George Wood all from my years at college, trauma surgeon Dr. James "Red" Duke, and Chaplain Rev. Dr. Julian Byrd at Memorial Hermann Hospital. Thank you all for teaching me two very important life skills: perseverance and resilience.

The definition of perseverance is the effort required to do something and keep doing it until the end, even if it's hard, to not give up, to have tenacity, persistence, to carry on, continue, keep on, plod on, keep going, be tenacious, to stand one's ground, fast and firm, to stay the course.

Thank you Mr. Piatz for claiming me as one of your boys. You made me feel proud.

I'm listening to the "Smile" lyrics again today to help me remember to smile and be strong. Please go look out for someone today. Smile and make life less hard and more beautiful for yourself and everyone around you.

MARCH 11, 2017
Saturday – MCFD#1 Pancake Breakfast
THE MCFD#1 PANCAKE BREAKFAST WAS GREAT fun for me. I love serving coffee, milk, and water to all the tables, talking with people, and working with the volunteers who are cooking the food for everyone.

While serving coffee and milk, I ran into a little girl named Liberty who had just fallen down outside on her way into the building. Her mom and aunt were with her and already had plates in hand but Liberty hadn't gotten anything yet so I offered to get her some chocolate milk. When I heard she had fallen down outside, I asked if I could help by looking at the abrasion on her knee. After checking

Liberty and me at the Marion County Fire District #1 Pancake Breakfast

it out, I went to a medic unit for an ice pack and broke it open to activate it for her. Then I gave her a plate of pancakes and checked on her throughout their time there.

As the hour passed, she was feeling better so we talked about Tinker Bell and I told her though I was out of Tinker Bell dust, I would give Tinker Bell a call to see if I could get some more. I now have some dust in the color she likes and will deliver it via hand-to-hand—first to the Fire Chief, then to his wife who knows Liberty's aunt, then to Liberty's mom, and then Liberty herself.

On their way out, I said good-bye and Liberty's mom looked so happy. Though her daughter had been upset after falling down, she was smiling and happy on her way out the door. Her mom even took our picture together.

MARCH 12, 2017
Sunday – MCFD#1 Pancake Breakfast

I ENJOYED THE BREAKFAST SO MUCH yesterday that I went back to help again today even though these were my two days off. While there, I met a retired volunteer Captain who had driven the display rig, a fire truck from the 1940s with a top speed of 45 mph.

Fire Chief Terry Riley and me.

Matt, Natalie, and Luke

My current paramedic partner from Medic 32 came. It was nice to see him and his family and we visited for a few minutes.

MARCH 17, 2017
Friday – St. Patrick's Day

I HAVE HAD ODOT, OTSC, AND Speed Zone meetings all week long. It's been fun to relax a bit for St. Patrick's Day today. To honor the holiday, I wore my kilt with my Irish FDNY T-shirt. Then on my way home, I stopped at Roth's and saw Darrell who hands out samples on Fridays and Kevin who runs the check stand. Darrell always finds something for me to buy from his samples and today I bought Dubliner cheese and Kevin checked me out. They are both so kind to me and I love that they both knew my mom and dad.

Darrell and me at Roth's

Kevin and me at Roth's

MARCH 23, 2017
Thursday

I AM AT ST. PAUL FIRE today and have already cleaned the toilets, sinks, mopped the floors, and cleaned out the refrigerator. The fridge, especially, was a mess. I took out all of the shelves and drawers and scrubbed it until it gleamed. After that, I checked out both ambulances.

The night I worked at MCFD#1 was busy with calls and transports the whole evening. In between the calls and writing the charts, I took out the garbage, cleaned the counters, and mopped the floor. At one point, I broke a coffee carafe while cleaning up so I bought a new one at the restaurant supply house in Salem yesterday to replace it.

MARCH 25, 2017
Saturday – Station 2, Medic 32

TODAY HAS BEEN A GOOD DAY with six different calls. First, I went down to Station 1 to check in the recent supply order in the EMS room. I couldn't find the packing slip so I used my spreadsheet list I make for every order instead. During a lull this evening, I walked on the treadmill, lifted small weights, and did sit-ups.

The first call we had today was my patient and when I gave my report to the nurse at the hospital, I noticed she was incredibly unhappy and had no smile at all. Though I knew her attitude wasn't about me, when we came through later, I noticed she still had the same stressed look while talking to a tech. She is the perfect example of why I smile, smile, and smile to see if my happiness can be shared to give joy to someone else's life and heart. So smile!

With all that is going on at County, I want to remind myself and you that we stay strong. Be resilient, persevere, endure, and stand firm.

Blessed is he who perseveres under trial because, having stood the test, that person will receive the crown of life that the Lord has promised to those who love him.

James 1:12

Please say a prayer for me tonight and I will say a prayer for you. We all have tests that seem so unfair and, in fact, are unfair, yet we have no choice but to persevere through all the pain and challenges of life. Every day, we see people who don't take up this challenge but drift into the abyss, slowly dying while ruining their lives and the lives of those around them. Please, help those who need your help. Show mercy and kindness. There are people who are trying so hard and struggling so much; please help them with their needs whether it's food, warm clothes and shoes, or their electric bill, and take the time to really see their struggles. Be that person who gives and shows love.

I know I've asked you for a lot thus far, but I want you to hold on and understand that hurt people have pain in their hearts. You've probably had a lot of hurt inside your own heart and soul. If you've had it in the past or are experiencing it now, then you understand and appreciate how a small amount of love and kindness can carry great meaning and how a person can be lifted up by small acts. Please, go out and show this love and kindness by helping those who are having ups and downs in their own lives. As others have helped you during your times of suffering and misfortune, seek out others you can help during their difficult times.

On the news this week, a high school boy was featured because he performed an abdominal thrust on another student who was choking. The news called him a hero for taking the training he had learned and putting it into practice at school. He *was* strong and *is* a hero. At the same time, there are other heroes who don't get special acclaim on the news. These heroes are heroes *every day*. As I have said before and will again, paramedics, EMTs, and firefighters are out doing their jobs for the community every single day of the year. Particularly those who work in ambulances never seem to get a thank you. You see many of them waiting on a street corner or in a parking lot for their next call as their office *is* their ambulance. This practice is called system status management and is the most evil thing invented by the ambulance industry. While waiting, these medics breathe in diesel fumes, have no bathrooms, and are expected to stand outside of their ambulances to stretch in the rain, heat, and snow. These paramedics are usually overworked, underpaid, and sometimes abused by their employers as well as their colleagues from the fire department in some parts of the country, even though they are all equal under the law and are all paramedics. Nursing staff often abuse the medics as well. What so many people don't understand is that we are all working together for the good of the sick and injured, yet some people have to put others down to make themselves feel superior.

Fire Chiefs, Emergency Directors, and private ambulance owners and managers: please stop the culture of hate and superiority and work together for the good of the community. If you demand perfection from the other agencies' medics, then why do you not demand the same high quality of care from your own people? It is time to treat all people equally. I know medics are treated like this from the reports of people from around the country and here at home. When I was on the Quality Improvement Committee, I would watch others slash and tear one of my medics apart about a call even though there were three paramedics on the call including theirs, not just mine. If it went wrong, it was my medic's fault and if a life was saved, it was to their medic's credit.

A few years ago, there was a terrible apartment fire where children were pulled out of a bathroom window in an attempt to save them from the fire. I was handed a little girl, about 6 years old, who was unconscious, limp, and barely breathing. Due to the extent of the damage and the number of victims, there was no help for me in the ambulance. So alone in the back, we transported the patient to the hospital via code 3, complete with red lights and sirens. I relied on every skill I had and by the time we arrived at the hospital, the girl was awake, breathing, talking to me, and had good muscle tone. When the celebration was held later on for saving the family's lives, we were not included.

Time to show love and charity to all of God's people

Two things then: first, could all health care workers just be courteous to each other and show respect to one another? Private ambulance medics *are* part of the team. Please be courteous and show mutual respect. Second, when you see an ambulance parked on a street corner or in a parking lot for an extended length of time, thank them for their service to the community. If you see them at the store buying food, smile, and tell them they are appreciated. Thank you.

It's now 11:26 p.m. and time to rest as we just got back from two calls. Thank you for being kind and showing charity to all. Good night.

MARCH 26, 2017
Sunday – Medic 32
IT'S BEEN A NICE NIGHT WITH no calls between midnight and 5:30 this morning so even though I woke up repeatedly, I slept fairly well.

This morning we had a call for a nice lady who has been unwell since August after having consulted multiple physicians. No one has been able to help her feel better or figure out what is causing her pain and today she was experiencing more pain than usual. After seeing so many physicians, she is incredibly frustrated to still have no answers or relief from the pain. We talked to her and she decided to not go to the emergency department but that she would see her doctor on Monday instead.

If you are going to church today, please find the person who no one talks to, someone who is struggling and who needs a smile. Give them that smile, some of Jesus' love, and be a blessing from the Holy Spirit. Be kind and show charity.

MARCH 27, 2017
Monday

IT'S NOW 1:58 A.M. ON MONDAY morning. We just got back from calls and I've already finished my charting and sent it to the hospital. My favorite nurses are working tonight. They are kind, helpful, and so understanding of the job we paramedics have to do.

I wanted to tell you about a "first" for my partner today. When it comes to firsts, I usually think about how many babies I've delivered. Today, though, Matt had his first ring cutting event! This happened when a call came in for a person who needed a ring cut off from their finger. When he told me this was his first, I thought about how many rings I've cut off of people throughout my career and it's just a few. I find it funny I've delivered more babies than cut off rings. I'm excited to have witnessed one of Matt's firsts!

One's best success comes after their greatest disappointments.
Harry Ward Beecher

I want to remind us all how lucky we are, even when things are difficult. Continue to have faith and hope and believe in the future. Show charity. Find beauty in everything, in every person you meet or talk with, or simply pass by, find their beauty and find the beauty within your own beautiful self. And smile!

No act of kindness, no matter how small, is ever wasted.

Aesop

March 29, 2017
Wednesday

I WENT TO A FUNERAL ON Monday for a Mt. Angel Fire Honorary. Clem Ruef was an awesome person and very good to me over the years. We took a fire truck and the rescue to both the church and cemetery to honor him and his work. At the funeral, they read the same scripture I placed on Mom's funeral card and it made me hope the same might be said about me someday. I was going to put the verse in the epilogue, but here it is for all of us to aspire to:

Well done, good and faithful servant.

Matthew 25:23

When I was younger, I played the pipe organ at St. Mary's Church for mass and for a wedding. Though I wasn't very good at it, it sure was fun at the time. My favorite "Angel" was there in stained glass next to the pipe organ. I took pictures of the window and printed them for a high school photography project. Today I took another and wanted to share it with you.

APRIL

APRIL 2, 2017

Sunday

WE'VE HAD AN AGGRAVATING AND BUSY two days. When I walked into the station at the beginning of the tour on Friday, the station was a mess and before I could clean it up, we got our first call.

One of our calls was for a 74 year old lady who fell in the driveway of her neighbor's house and hit her head. I'd talked to the other medics on the scene and asked if they thought she should be a trauma entry. They didn't think she needed it but with repetitive questioning, I determined she had retrograde amnesia. To start, I gave her a list to remember which she couldn't recall but instead told me she was scared as she held on to me and asked my name. I told her my name then asked her to repeat the list I gave her. She couldn't do it so I asked her my name instead and with a gleam in her eye and a smile on her face, she answered, "good looking." With that response alone I knew she should be a trauma entry! At the hospital, she got a trauma team response and an immediate CAT scan. I heard later she had multiple subarachnoid bleeds and was admitted to the hospital.

On Saturday we were told I was moving permanently to a different station at the beginning of the next shift. The news was disappointing to both Matt and I for multiple reasons. Plus, I had already worked on finding someone to come in early for me next Saturday.

I need to follow my own advice to others when circumstances like these occur. There is the quote from Romans 8:28 so often heard when something goes wrong: "God causes all things to work together for good…" which for me is better translated as "all things work together for good." Still, I don't see this as God making the change, but life being life and placing these difficulties upon us. All of humankind has things fall upon them that are not good, or right, or happy.

I believe that good can be found not in what happens *to* us, but in how we *respond* to the challenges life gives us. As an example, in 2009, Victor 3 died and this was and remains terribly hard for me. My first day back at work after his funeral, I had a call for a man who was highly intoxicated in the middle of the day. I got him into the ambulance and started to take care of him by starting an intravenous line for a fluid bolus of normal saline to help him feel better. While I did so, he told me his wife left him because he was drinking. As I listened to him telling me how difficult his life was for him, I thought of my son's recent death and considered whether I should start drinking myself or continue to cope and be strong. I am choosing every day to be strong but it's not easy. Every one of us has this choice to make: we can react by being strong and moving forward or lose ourselves in numbness and addiction. It seems that whatever choice I make, though, it's a difficult road for me and I deal with the stress and frustration of it either way.

Today I have the same choice to make here at the Fire District. I am moving to Station 1 and Matt is staying at Station 2. Over the time I've known him these last three months, he's helped me so much by teaching me computer skills and assisting me with the stocking of and checking off incoming supply orders in the EMS room. He's been so good to me and has looked out for my welfare. He even tells me I teach him new skills. How surprising! Matt is a very smart and hardworking man.

So I'll go to the Four Corners Station and make my mark there as I work hard at my EMS room project and taking care of the patients.

Goodnight and find peace within yourself.

April 7, 2017
Friday

It's Friday afternoon and this is the first chance I've had to sit down and write.

Yesterday started with a meeting then we ran calls all day and throughout the night, 13 so far. There was a wind storm this morning and there must have been over 50 calls for wires down throughout Marion County. At least two houses had trees fall on them in addition to multiple crashes resulting from traffic lights being out of order. It's now 5:23 p.m. and we have a lot of charts to write. Especially on days like this, I feel compelled to work hard on taking care of people and being strong. I'm not sure what is in me giving me the drive to show compassion, respect, and care for people, but that compassion for excellent service is there just the same.

Perhaps the answer is in this verse from 2 Corinthians: "For Christ's love compels us…" I rely upon God for strength and wisdom. A Sister from the Benedictine Convent in Mount Angel taught me to pray, "May the precious blood of Jesus protect me, guide me, keep me safe, grant me strength, and give me knowledge and wisdom, and allow my experience and skills to come through to help me help others." I know the job I do is nearly impossible yet somehow, by the grace of God, I continue to give it my best. Thank you Almighty God and Father, Son, and Holy Spirit.

I'm going to stop writing now so I can finish my charts before we get more calls. Pray for me and for all the paramedics, EMTs, and firefighters out there doing their jobs serving their communities.

April 8, 2017
Saturday

On my way to Portland at 5:00 a.m., I was incredibly thankful to Aaron for coming in early so I wouldn't be late to the Expo Center to work medical standby. I had just finished my last chart at 4:30 a.m., just in time to clean up, shave, and change into my uniform.

I asked myself if I was actually living up to *Semper Fortis*. Forty-eight hours earlier, I started my tour of duty and did not stop moving, working, or writing charts. Having arrived at 6:27 a.m., we were soon heading to our first meeting scheduled for 7:30 at College Station. By 8:30, we got our first call and started caring for the people in our community. It wasn't until late in the evening that we stopped for a brief break and I ate some rice for dinner before going back out on calls throughout the night and into the early morning. After getting back to the station around 5:00 a.m., another gigantic wind storm came up and we ran calls until noon then had a slice of toast for lunch before heading out again. The calls didn't slow down until 10:00 p.m. which was just long enough for Matt and I to trade stations so that Aaron could come in early for me on Sunday morning as the person at the Four Corners Station couldn't come in 90 minutes early. After we traded, we had three more calls, in between which, I worked on writing the charts until I finished at 4:30 a.m. All told, we had 18 calls and transported to both Silverton and Salem Hospitals. It feels like a blur now, but I know we took care of numerous patients with shortness of breath, addictions to methamphetamines, strokes, motor vehicle crashes, a chest pain patient, and a trauma entry.

I love what I am doing and I want to continue running around all day and night taking care of people. This year alone, Matt and I've had a code save and Ashley and I had our Thanksgiving Day baby delivery. It's so much fun and I take great joy in helping others, touching lives, and giving hope and peace to people.

I believe I've proved my value and worth by not only the excellent care and treatment I provide to my patients, but also through my hard work and diligence in cleaning, mopping, and emptying the garbage at the stations. I've also worked hard on improving the disposable medical supplies system and the medication management and ordering system. I know you pray for me and believe in me yet here I am with doubts, misgivings, and a fear of the future. I'm still feeling disappointed about the move. I was so hoping to stay at County the rest of my active career.

Semper Fortis is sometimes used as a motto in the Navy and means, "Always Strong" or "Always Courageous." I had hoped that I was strong and courageous. I've stepped into burning buildings in my younger days and even now, I regularly walk into unknown situations to treat the sick and injured. If you have not yet lost total faith in me, would you please pray I am still able to do what I love with passion, to take care of people, and to do so at County?

All this said, I am still the 63 year old probie. Nick Ottele from Salem Fire saw me last night while on a call and he loves to hear me call myself the probie. All the staff at Salem Fire are good to me; they give me both respect and courtesy, especially Nick and the engine crew at Station 8. (Nick, myself, and a team of medics were on a code save in 2014 for which we all received the Red Cross Everyday Heroes Award.) He laughs at me, in a fond way, while I'm mopping the floors and emptying the garbage for he's seen me provide superior and excellent pre-hospital care in the field. Yes, saving lives, delivering babies, holding a little old lady's hand, and giving comfort is a tough job but somebody has to do it. Thank goodness we are part of that excellence.

April 9, 2017
Sunday

Today is Palm Sunday and I've been feeling discouraged. Mom's birthday was the 6th of April and it's been a long year without her here. Then, these last few days, I've been dealing with the threat of being let go from where I like to work and no longer being able to do what I love. So today I opened up my Bible and looked at the program from Victor 3's funeral where I was reminded of my favorite song: "It Is Well with My Soul." Listening to the song on YouTube as well as "Amazing Grace" and "On Christ the Solid Rock I Stand" was very comforting.

I've talked before about Dietrich Bonhoeffer's view of having Christ-like suffering in our lives. I was born with birth defects and have struggled with them since birth, particularly with getting past other people's *perceptions* of my disability. On so many occasions, I've been told no and being told no is why I went to law school so I could fight for myself and others. Now, after loving people my entire life, I have allowed myself to become disheartened and I'm disappointed in myself.

The version of "It Is Well with My Soul" I found on YouTube was sung by Wintley Phipps. He is a wonderful singer and before he began, he said this, "It is in the quiet crucible of your personal, private sufferings, that your noblest dreams are born and God's greatest gifts are given in compensation for what you have been through."

The song was written by Horatio G. Spafford and I love the story of how he came to be inspired to create it. The story reminds me to be strong and courageous.

When peace, like a river, attendeth my way,
When sorrows like sea billows roll;
Whatever my lot, Thou hast taught me to say,
It is well, it is well with my soul.

Chorus:
It is well with my soul,
It is well, it is well with my soul.

Horatio G. Spafford was a successful lawyer and businessman in Chicago with a lovely family—a wife, Anna, and five children. However, they were not strangers to tears and tragedy. Their young son died from pneumonia in 1871 and in that same year, much of their business was lost in the great Chicago fire. Yet, God in His mercy and kindness allowed the business to flourish once more.

On November 21, 1873, the French ocean liner, Ville du Havre, was crossing the Atlantic from the U.S. to Europe with 313 passengers on board. Among the passengers were Mrs. Spafford and their four daughters. Although Mr. Spafford had planned to go with his family, he found it necessary to stay in Chicago to help solve an unexpected business problem. He told his wife he would join her and their children in Europe a few days later by taking another ship.

About four days into the crossing of the Atlantic, the Ville du Harve collided with a powerful, iron-hulled Scottish ship, the Loch Earn. Suddenly, all of those on board were in grave danger. Anna hurriedly brought her four children to the deck. She knelt there with Annie, Margaret Lee, Bessie, and Tanetta to pray that God would spare them if that could be His will, or to make them willing to endure whatever awaited them. Within approximately 12 minutes, the Ville du Harve slipped beneath the dark waters of the Atlantic, carrying with it 226 of the passengers including the four Spafford children.

A sailor, rowing a small boat over the spot where the ship went down, spotted a woman floating on a piece of the wreckage. It was Anna, still alive. He pulled her into the boat and they were picked up by another large vessel, which, nine days later, landed them in Cardiff, Wales. From there, she wired her husband a message which began, "Saved alone, what shall I do?" Mr. Spafford later framed the telegram and placed it in his office.

Another of the ship's survivors, Pastor Weiss, later recalled Anna saying, "God gave me four daughters. Now they have been taken from me. Someday, I will understand why."

Mr. Spafford booked passage on the next available ship and left to join his grieving wife. With the ship about four days out, the captain called Spafford to his cabin and told him they were over the place where his children went down.

According to Bertha Spafford Vester, a daughter born after the tragedy, Spafford wrote "It Is Well with My Soul" while on this journey.

When peace like a river attendeth my way,
When sorrows like sea billows roll,
Whatever my lot, thou hast taught me to say,
It is well, it is well with my soul.

Chorus:
It is well with my soul,
It is well, it is well with my soul.

Victor's funeral program, prayer card, and Victor, Paul, and myself at
Paul's graduation, 2007

I have so many dreams of doing awesome things for people and
my community. I am not sure how to get there, but I keep dream-
ing. If I could only have one dream left in me, it would be to keep
doing what I am doing right now at Mt. Angel Fire and Marion
County Fire.

I walked through a swap meet today and found such kindness
from all the vendors. A man I know, Danny Carlson, was selling toy
cars and he gave me a toy fire truck. I tried to pay him but he just said
to me, "Thanks for what you do and just keep doing it." Amazing!!!

His kindness lifted my heart and spirit and gave me the courage to, once again, continue trying and believing and, most of all, smiling.

APRIL 12, 2017
Wednesday

GOOD AFTERNOON, IT IS EXACTLY 5:00 p.m. and we just finished writing our charts. Luckily, I already completed the EMS order. Though I'm out of a couple items, I chose not to spend the extra money to have it shipped via two day ground.

Our calls today have been for chest pain and a MVC plus our regular drills. I argued my case this morning with a Union negotiator about paying paramedics an appropriate amount and not just trying to get more money for themselves. I just need to relax and not worry about it.

All of us have to climb over these obstacles. If everything was smooth and level, there would be no mountains to climb or hills

to walk and hike on. We all have to have faith and get through the struggles.

We should focus on helping others this week and always. This is how we know what love is: Jesus Christ laid down his life for us and in that same way, we ought to lay down our lives for our brothers and sisters. We ought to love each other and help the less fortunate, the poor, the hungry, the disenfranchised, and those who need understanding and not our judgment. We should be inclusive and not exclusive by welcoming all and judging no one.

The Friends church I am a part of has been dealing with questions. Though we are trying to welcome all people into the church, we are asking ourselves how to do that? Everyone agrees everyone should be welcomed into the church but membership is different than attendance since one must accept and believe the tenets of the faith to be a member. I think we should love all who cross over the threshold of our churches, warmly welcoming them and inviting them back to our churches again and again. We are all God's children. Jesus loved

April 12, 2017

us when we were yet sinners. Show God's love. You see, at just the right time, when we were still powerless, Christ died for the ungodly. God demonstrates his own love for us in this: "While we were still sinners, Christ died for us." (Romans 5)

The New Testament church was built on helping the community, the widows, and the orphans. They fed and helped everyone no matter who they were for all need the love of God revealed to them by those of us who know the love of God personally. In the same way, we, too, ought to demonstrate His love by helping others, to be inclusive, to be generous to the disadvantaged, and open our doors to all.

April 13, 2017
Thursday

Good morning. It's 1:19 a.m. and we have just returned from a motor vehicle crash. I don't know how to get the message across to people about the dangers of drinking alcohol and driving. Just don't drink

No matter how you feel, get up, dress up, show up and never give up.

anything and then drive! Being safe on the roadways is *so* important for everyone. The woman in the crash whom we treated isn't making it home to her little girl tonight and even after she is released from the hospital, she'll probably be going to jail for driving while intoxicated. The fallout from this will be devastating to both her and her family. Just don't drink at all. Stay home with your family and love them.

I just came from the hospital where I got to see Peter, the Assistant Nurse Manager; Angie, the Charge Nurse; and Lane, who is PFC today. They are always kind to me and it's great to see them for they constantly give me hope and encouragement.

By the next call, the crew had changed at the hospital so Hattie was at the PFC desk along with Stacey and Ann. Just like the earlier team, they are awesome people and wonderful nurses. Whenever I'm there and see them, they are incredibly nice and good to me. Thank you all for being great, amazing, and so kind.

The last patient I had was a 76 year old woman who was having chest pain for the past four days. I started an IV and told her I didn't think I was getting any Easter presents as I was successful on the first try. She told me her veins roll so she'd said a prayer to which I smiled and replied that I had too!

It's been a long tour for me. After all the calls, I put away two orders of supplies and medications then Eli and I emptied the garbage, mopped the floors, and started the dishwasher while the Captain cleaned the kitchen counters. It's now time for a nap and, hopefully, some sleep.

♦♦♦

Back at the Salem Hospital Emergency Department, I got to see Chuck and Stephanie before the end of my shift. They are both excellent Charge Nurses and managers. The whole team have difficult jobs, especially when you consider all the patients they see on a daily basis. Wanting to do something kind for them, I dropped

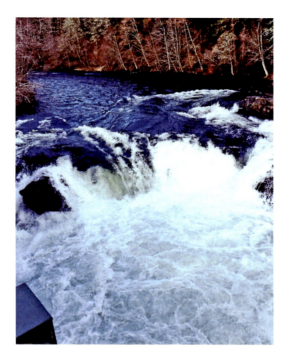

off some treats in the nurses' lounge for the staff this morning and saw Nancy Bee while I was there. I can't say Nancy Bee's first name without saying her last name at the same time, it flows so smoothly. She's an awesome Assistant Nurse Manager with whom I worked on the Quality Improvement Committee for six years. Nancy Bee is extremely intelligent and understands what we as paramedics do in the field. She's always looked out for me and been my advocate.

Two of my other favorite people are Richard and Stacy who are both hardworking, dedicated, and bright Med Techs at the hospital. Both of them are committed to their patients and their fellow staff. Thank you for being here and working so extremely hard, always greeting me with your kind words and incredible smiles. All these people lift my heart and soul.

APRIL 15, 2017
Saturday

MY FRIEND LARRY ANDRES IS VERY sick at the Oregon Health & Science University up in Portland so I headed up there early this morning to visit with him at the hospital. When I arrived, I saw his family sitting outside of his ICU room. They instructed me to "gown up" so I could go in and talk with him for a few minutes. Though he's sedated and comatose, I talked to him as if he could hear every word I said. We were on the ambulance and at the Mt. Angel Fire Department together and he was very close to my dad when they ran the ambulance before my dad died in 1991. I thanked him for all he had done and told him how much I appreciated it.

Larry made a huge difference in my life. Before 1980, we had no ambulance in Mt. Angel and Dad decided we should have one. So with the help of Woodburn Ambulance, we were able to get the equipment and gather the needed volunteers through the fire department. Between Larry, my dad, Clem, Norb, Don, Jack, Denny, Dave, and myself, we would all get up and respond to anything and everything. If we transported someone to the hospital, we received 50 cents and the ambulance would then bill for the transport.

One afternoon, Larry, Dave Welton, and I were on the ambulance when we got a call for a woman in labor. When we arrived, the woman was in the back of a van with her baby coming, which turned out to be her thirteenth child. The three of us caught the baby, cleaned her up, dried her, and cut the cord before taking them to the hospital. It was the first delivery for all of us.

Out of all the charter members, Larry and I were the last two left to still be doing the job. Larry recently retired and, as you know, I am still here doing my best.

♦♦♦

I AM NOW AT THE OREGON Convention Center running medical standby for two events. While doing my usual walk around, I ran into a woman who greeted me by name, gave me a hug, and told me how nice it was to see me again. She's a vendor I've seen before at other events and so I walked with her to her booth while we talked about her boyfriend and her recent promotion. I thanked her for remembering my name and she asked me to say hello again before the show was over so I made sure to stop by before the end of the day. I love working here as people are so kind to me. Please go out and be kind to someone. You will never know how much that kindness means to the other person.

APRIL 16, 2017
Easter Sunday
I'M LISTENING TO THE SONG, "THE Blood Will Never Lose its Power" by Andraé Crouch. As you know, I've been struggling all year. Of course, my issues are easy compared to people like Larry, people struggling with sickness, death, poverty, homelessness, and so many other awful

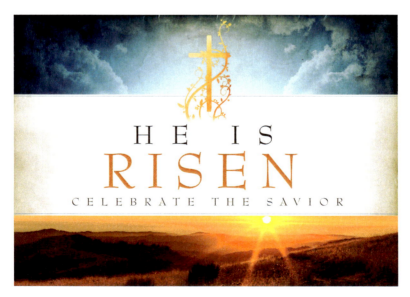

situations. Yet, I *am* human and have feelings of sadness and loss just like anyone else. Today on this Easter Sunday, I am renewing my faith and hope. Let's join together and be strong while serving others with a smile. You keep praying for me and I will keep praying for you.

THE BLOOD WILL NEVER LOSE ITS POWER
Andraé Crouch

Verse 1:
The blood that Jesus shed for me,
way back on Calvary;
the blood that gives me strength
from day to day,
it will never lose its power.

Chorus:
It reaches to the highest mountain,
and it flows to the lowest valley;
the blood that gives me strength
from day to day,
it will never lose its power.

Verse 2:
It soothes my doubts and calms my fears,
and it dries all my tears;
the blood that gives me strength
from day to day,
it will never lose its power.

Chorus:
It reaches to the highest mountain,
and it flows to the lowest valley;
the blood that gives me strength

from day to day,
it will never lose its power.

Let's all find strength. Feel the power.

We should first find peace in ourselves and forgive others, then pass that peace on to the world by showing love and charity. We ought to be helping the widows and orphans and feeding the poor. No one should have to deal with homelessness or not have the medicine or heat they need. Be inclusive, not exclusive, while showing the love of God to all His children. Pass on to them hope and peace while showing love, understanding, compassion, and kindheartedness. Forgive.

Saint Mary's Church, Mount Angel, Oregon

APRIL 18, 2017
Tuesday

LARRY DIED OVER THE WEEKEND. WE'VE worked together, side-by-side, since 1980 on both the ambulance and at the fire department. Over all those years, he saved many lives and served the community without fanfare. He will be sorely missed, especially by me.

Yesterday, I came over to Marion County to check in one of my supply orders. It was a large one including liter bags of Normal

Saline along with numerous other supplies and medications we desperately need to have available on the crews' shelves. A second order had also arrived but before I could check it in and unpack it this morning, we had to rush off to a call in Aumsville.

Larry Andres and Michelle

When we answered the call at the care home in Aumsville, we found a man experiencing severe back pain. Fortunately, Aumsville Fire had been kind enough to place an IV before we got there. It saved a ton of time for us and enabled us to treat him right away by administering Fentanyl for his pain as we took him to Santiam Memorial Hospital. Both the Fire Department crew and the hospital staff were incredibly kind and took wonderful care of our patient.

♦♦♦

SOMEONE CALLED ME FOR LEGAL ADVICE yesterday. Almost every week, someone in Oregon calls me for some kind of legal assistance. Between all the firefighters, EMTs, paramedics, and other health professionals, I keep getting referrals. I'm always glad to help if I can or, if I can't, I refer them to other lawyers I know. These phone calls remind me of the many lawyers who have helped me whenever I have a question. I enjoy being able to return the favor to others. One of the people I ask for advice is Ryan Collier. Ryan does estate planning and has actually done some pro bono work for one of my clients as it was more complicated than my expertise can cover.

The other two lawyers I frequently consult are John J. Tyner III and John Henry Hingson III who are always willing to help me whenever I need it. Both men are extremely intelligent, committed to justice, and are amazing lawyers. They both mean a great deal to me and I am deeply appreciative of them.

I was once working a case in Washington County where I didn't know the system so Tyner helped with the paperwork and then called the District Attorney to help resolve the issue. He helped me look good professionally and we won the battle.

Right after Victor 3 died, Hingson and I were at the same conference. While I was sitting by a door waiting to go into an event, he walked by with an entourage who were listening to his every word. They looked like a bunch of puppies following the dad dog around in order to learn as much as possible from him. Seeing me, he suddenly stopped, turned back, came over to me, and took my hand and asked if I was okay while extending his condolences. Even with all of those people around him, he took the time to stop in the middle of it all to check on me! Both of these men are terrific people and wonderful friends.

THE LAST TWO CALLS WE RESPONDED to today were for patients and their families who have a plethora of issues: social, domestic, and physical. Even with all we are going through, we are fortunate. I feel thankful today for my struggles for they are nothing compared to the suffering Larry went through, the suffering his family is going through right now, and the suffering of all the families we worked with today.

APRIL 19, 2017
Wednesday

WE HAD A GOOD NIGHT AND didn't have our first call until 6:58 this morning when we treated a diabetic patient with a glucose level of 599. After taking him to the hospital, I grabbed a snack back at the station before we headed to College Station for a drill.

In our culture, our favorite TV shows are often those about a character seeking justice for another. Whether it's *Perry Mason,*

Metal Matchbox ambulance made in England

NCIS, Columbo, or any number of other shows, they all intrigue us as the characters seek justice. We all want justice and should seek it for everyone around us. I remember what my professor told us in law school, "This is law school, not fair school. Fair school is down the street, this is law school." In the world, people are murdered by governments, terrorists, and crazy people. Some governments starve their people to build bombs and threaten other nations. What do we do? For me, we are to help those people we can touch today. I am lucky to have a career of helping people as a paramedic, lawyer, and hospital chaplain. When I was a child, I would be pulled into a room at Good Samaritan Hospital to hold the hands of kids there for the first time or to push people around in their wheelchairs. I would even help feed other small children after I ate to help the nurses. In grade school, I volunteered at the nursing home in town.

That is why I am so happy about being with MCFD#1: I get to do what I want to do with my life. Plus, I get added responsibilities such as managing supplies and medications and I hope to receive more responsibilities. Though I do get tired and it's difficult for me some-times, this is the best place for me to achieve my goals of serving the community. Plus, I get to serve my community with Mt. Angel Fire.

APRIL 22, 2017
Saturday

I AM AT THE EXPO CENTER today doing medical standby and I want to tell you about something amazing that happened. The Performance Warehouse Trade Show is going on and while I walked past the booths and displays visiting with vendors, one of them asked if I was having lunch there. When I said no, that I don't do that at the Expo Center, he told me to go get a lunch ticket. A few hours later, the vendor saw me and gave me a lunch ticket they'd obtained on my behalf and insisted in the strongest terms that I go eat. I was quite touched by their thoughtfulness and told the vendor thank you.

Do you realize that in all the years I've done standbys that I've never known anyone to worry about the medics? People worry about the stars, the talent, and the staff, but never the medics. How thoughtful and courteous they were to me! (I've always wanted to be at some gigantic event and find the medics to make sure that they were well taken care of.)

I ATTENDED THE DUII MDT CONFERENCE this week and Jack Enter, Ph.D., spoke about leadership. He was a wonderful speaker and centered his talk on the proactive leadership strategies of law enforcement. There was only one part of his talk I would have changed—I would have added a whole section about servant leadership. As the 63 year old Probie, I'm proud of working hard and doing my job, including doing simple chores like emptying the garbage and mopping the floor. I haven't wanted to be lazy and I don't think of my years of experience as giving me a pass to perform chores around the station. I remember a text from one firefighter who, after just one week on the job as a firefighter, clearly stated he was a firefighter now and therefore far above the single role paramedic!

I prefer to lead by not only doing my job but by regularly going above and beyond. It is what I am doing *today* that matters. Paramedics are challenged to perform at their best on every single call. That's what I have always tried to do. I am going to work even harder at leading—to lead by being a servant, by caring about both patients and colleagues, and by being an example of good paramedicine. To do this, I will work on skills like self-awareness, forgiveness, and fairness, and I will remember that what I do *does* make a difference. Do you remember that what you do makes a difference?

Together, let's continue to make a difference. Let's forgive, be fair, and lead by helping others. Stop talking and start walking. Be a servant. Show compassion and love and charity.

April 24, 2017
Monday
Today I'm at Station 1, Medic 31, and I'm looking forward to a great tour. Bret Peterson is covering the engineer position on Engine 315 today which will be fun. He enjoys giving me a difficult time and I usually give it right back to him. He usually works B shift and considers me a B shifter as well since that's where I started before

being reassigned. Seaton was also here and I got to say hello before he went off duty. I enjoyed working with them on B shift for when they work together, it's like putting gasoline and heat together—you get fire!

We received a call for a 20 year old woman who had swallowed glass, metal, and plastic, with resulting abdominal pain. Our next call was for a woman needing CPR. This one made me sad as the woman was already dead. She already had rigor and lividity as well as being cold to the touch. Her daughter was distraught as she had found her that way when she came over for a morning visit. The mom was only 51 years old. I asked if they had a church, which they did, so I called to ask the pastor to come over and he said he was on his way. Our third call was for a 20 year old man with kidney stones. I gave him Fentanyl for pain while he told me he drinks 3 gallons of milk and lots of sports drinks every week. I suggested to him that the combination of the calcium in the milk and the sodium in the sports drinks may be contributing to his kidney stones and suggested he ask his physician about it.

When we returned from the third call, we had drill for two hours before taking more calls and catching up on our charts. In the evening, Eli gave an excellent lecture and demonstrated the Holmatro extrication tool.

After everyone ate, Bret, Eli, and I sat in the charting office for a while talking about striving for excellence in EMS and the contrast between being an EMS executive chef rather than a cookbook medic. A cookbook medic doesn't think for themselves and just follows the protocol. In contrast, the executive chef medic is able to reason with critical thinking skills and is the superior caregiver. It was nice to talk to other medics who understand this concept of thinking critically and caring for people with the goal of practicing excellent medicine.

It's almost midnight now but before I try to sleep, I wanted to tell you what happened at the hospital. I was heading out with the stretcher when I saw my friend Ann working as the charge nurse for the night. We talked for a few moments and she could sense I'd had a long day so she came around from behind the desk to give me a hug and remind me that I am one of her favorite medics and a favorite of all of the staff. I thanked her for telling me that to which she smiled and assured me I really am one of her favorites. That brought a tear to my eye. How awesome is that for her to tell me I am appreciated? I am truly grateful for her kind actions and loving words. Thank you again, Ann, and thank you to all of the great team who take care of those patients and are so good to me.

APRIL 25, 2017
Tuesday

IT WAS MIDNIGHT BY THE TIME we got done last night and were able to get some rest for a couple of hours before an incoming call at 4:37 a.m. The call was for a very sick elderly woman with chronic obstructive pulmonary disease (COPD) in near respiratory failure due to her blocked air passages. I was ready to CPAP her, which I usually don't do for COPD patients due to the fragility of their lungs. When we got her onto the stretcher, I decided to go Code 3 to the hospital so we could get there quickly. On our way, I started an IV, gave her two

Duo Neb treatments, and a dose of Dexamethasone. By the time we arrived, she was still sick but improved and I felt grateful to have been able to help her. Brent came in with me to help care for her which I very much appreciated.

At 7:35 a.m., we had a headache call that was really a severe hypertensive crisis. In addition, the beta blockers she had been taking for her headaches weren't working for her headaches but were instead slowing her heart rate down to the 40s! I treated her with some Fentanyl for her headache, just in case we could relieve some of the pain and the corresponding elevated blood pressure.

Larry's funeral is Friday and I will be there to support Shelly. The Mt. Angel Fire District is planning to participate as well by taking an engine and the rescue. I visited with Shelly on Sunday night and she was doing better. It is a great blow to lose a loved one and she has lost two: her Uncle Clem died three weeks ago and now her husband Larry, the two closest people to her. Shelly shared with me a photo of Larry, my dad, and Larry's dad from the Oktoberfest many years ago.

Vic Hoffer, Larry, and George Andres

WHAT A DAY! IT'S GONE BY so fast. We have just finished cleaning the station—I mopped, Eli vacuumed, and the TODs emptied the garbage cans.

At lunch I choked on some food and it took me a while to clear my throat. Shortly afterwards, we got a call for someone else who was choking. When we arrived, we found an elderly lady who had been given a huge pill which got stuck in her esophagus. I comforted and reassured her while we had her sip on water so the pill could dissolve enough to go down the rest of the way. It really hurts when something gets stuck. Engine 10 responded along with me and let me handle the situation and comfort the patient. After we cleared the call, the Captain told me they would take care of the charting. The Engine 10 crew was made up of Captain Trevor Elmer, engineer Brandon Silence, and firefighter Matt Shore. They are all excellent paramedics and I have worked with them for about 10 years now and we have always worked well together.

After that, we had an amazing call! An eight year old girl had been playing on her bed when she fell off and landed on the leg of a metal rack laying upside down on the floor. The leg was five inches long and every inch was impaled into her abdomen. We found her on the floor with her mom holding her head when we arrived.

I introduced myself by telling her my name as I got down on the floor with her. She told me it hurt and I said I was sorry. She then shared that she was scared and I assured her I would stay with her the whole time, that I would not leave her, and that her mom could go to the hospital with us. I also added that, if she wanted, I would be her Grandpa Victor for the next little bit. In response, she squeezed my hand tight and said "Okay." We made her a trauma entry and headed to the hospital with red lights and sirens blaring. Bret Peterson, my engineer and fellow paramedic, and Brandon Hari, my TOD, rode in with us and we stabilized her and the rack along the way. At the hospital, they wanted to get a wire cutter to cut the rack but I looked up from kneeling on the floor, eye level with my patient, and said, "No, we will get the bolt cutter out of the medic." We all knew it would work far better so Bret retrieved the tool and did a perfect job cutting off the wire rack. When we got into the trauma bay in the hospital, I stayed with her as promised and talked to her for a long time. Eventually, her mom was guided over and I stepped back for her to take over for me.

Sometimes there are obstacles in the way of progress. We will just have to have faith and get over, under, or around them.

APRIL 26, 2017
Wednesday

IT'S WEDNESDAY NOW AND WE JUST got back from the hospital. I am told the little girl will be fine. All the important organs were missed by the steel leg impaled into her side. We are so thankful and I am thankful for all the help from my colleagues and from Heaven above that made things go so well. God gives me knowledge and skill and I believe that Dad and Victor 3 are looking out for me as well.

Victor Jeremiah Hoffer, born April 26, 1977, died January 2, 2009

My son, Victor Hoffer, was a superb human being and a total giver. He helped everyone and endured injustice doing it. A believer in both God and country, he believed in the hearts of those around him. Victor 3 was the ultimate officer and gentleman. Today he enjoys the beauty of Heaven. The poem "Success" by Ralph Waldo Emerson was Victor's belief and motto.

One of Victor's favorite photographs. He took it capturing the missile in mid-air while he served as an Army officer of a Patriot Missile battery. He would have been 40 years old today.

SUCCESS
Ralph Waldo Emerson

To laugh often and much;
to win the respect of intelligent people and
the affection of honest critics and
endure the betrayal of false friends;
to appreciate beauty, to find the best in others;
to leave the world a bit better;

> *whether by a healthy child,*
> *a garden patch or a redeemed social condition*
> *to know even one life has breathed easier because you have lived.*
> *This is to have succeeded.*

APRIL 28, 2017
Friday

LARRY'S FUNERAL WAS TODAY. WE TOOK both an engine and rescue to represent his work with the fire department. Silverton Fire, Woodburn Fire, and Woodburn Ambulance all brought their vehicles as well. Between all of us, we had a great procession to the cemetery. The funeral reminded me how we must all show love and charity every day. "It Is Well with My Soul" was played and I quietly sang the words under my breath while shedding tears for Larry, Dad, and Victor 3. The loss of all three leaves me feeling sorrowful and my heart is heavy as I remind myself we must never lose our compassion and our ability to feel another's pain along with our own.

I'm blessed to still be able to work out in the field taking care of people. Most of my colleagues from the 1980s are no longer working with the patients. Some are managers and others have retired. Matt says he'll retire before me and I'll just keep going and going. Matt really understands me, my passion for what I do best, and my desire to not stop. Lord, please give me strength and keep me strong.

God loves us all—everyone—yes, everyone. He loves *all* of his children. The love of God surpasses all human understanding. I am so concerned that some churches are not inclusive. They want to exclude and are so biased, prejudiced, and judgmental. How about we just show the love of God for His children to all? When a person comes to church, show them the love of God. Don't shut them out! Please, please, yes please, love *all* people, help *all* people. Show the understanding you want from others and help as you would want to be helped in your time of need. Throughout this journal, I have talked a lot about the destitute, the disenfranchised, and the poor and we *must* take the extra steps to find those people and help them. Help the widows and orphans, help your neighbor, be a real friend and help them. We must be inclusive to *all* the community; we really must show love and understanding. It is time for us all to be instruments of God's love. Please, be inclusive to all of God's children!

♦♦♦

WHAT IS A LEADER? A REAL leader has many traits, yet I believe there are some key characteristics which truly define someone who does leadership well. These are the traits I'm reaching for and want to accomplish. First, the leader is truly the servant. My dad served his firefighters when he was Fire Chief. He looked out for them and did all he could to make their lives easier. The leader-servant takes care of his or her people and truly cares about them and their families. For me, I am trying to care for my colleagues by having the EMS room stocked and easy to navigate when they are tired, need supplies, and just want to go back to their station to get some rest. I am buying supplies that will make their job easier and that are better for the patient. If I can help cover for my fellow medics, assist the firefighters, or do anything else to make their lives easier, I am ready. I even bring in goodies. I know that doesn't seem very special, but a good chocolate chip cookie or some Red Vines when you are tired can be so uplifting and fun.

A leader-servant also leads by example. Eli is working hard to keep the station cleaned up since he is the new firefighter. I am working hard to not let him do it all. During our last tour together, I sneaked the garbage out, mopped the kitchen floor, and took care of 8 out of the 11 patients we were called to help.

I am doing my best to learn about myself in this new situation and I am so thankful to be here at MCFD#1. Though I worry I'll be let go under the new system, I am working hard to be self-aware and hyper-vigilant. What we do at Marion County Fire truly does make a difference.

We have made it through the funeral, the memories, the sadness, and the joy of God's promise. All afternoon I have been listening to the song, "Precious Lord, Take My Hand," by Thomas A. Dorsey. It gives me comfort.

> *Precious Lord, take my hand*
> *Lead me on, Let me stand*
> *I'm tired, I am weak, I am worn*
> *Through the storm, through the night*
> *Lead me home to the light*
> *Take my hand precious Lord, lead me home*

Be a leader-servant, show love and compassion, help others, forgive, and care about your friends, family, and community.

April 30, 2017
Sunday

Good Morning! We started the morning off with a call at 6:54 a.m. for a transport to Salem Hospital Emergency Department. (SHED) When I walked into the hospital, Peter, Angie, and Lane were all there. They're so great and I felt relieved to see them knowing they are here all day. All three are kind, compassionate, caring, and are a pleasure to work with. Whenever I call in to give my notification report, they trust what I tell them. Whether I have a very sick patient or someone who is actually doing pretty well, they understand and respect what I say when I tell them what they should be prepared to do for them. All in all, it's been an excellent morning. I got to see my colleagues at SHED and when we got back, I went to the weight room to work out for a short while before eating some leftovers.

Peter, Angie, me, and Lane on April 30, 2017

MAY

MAY 1, 2017
Monday

WE WERE BUSY ALL DAY AND night long and now I'm hoping to write a few notes before we get another call. First, I'm off to get some ice cream.

MAY 2, 2017
Tuesday

THE FIRE CHIEF CAME IN YESTERDAY to tell me the mom of the girl who had been impaled called to tell us her daughter was doing well and to say thank you for taking such wonderful care of her. I reminded the Chief that Bret and Brandon were there with me and that her successful care was a team effort.

We then had a call from the dialysis center for a patient who was having chest pain and shortness of breath. We did all the things we're supposed to do for chest pain including administering aspirin, nitroglycerin, and oxygen and we obtained a 12-lead EKG tracing. I thought that it looked like a STEMI with elevation in V1, V2, V3 and V4 with depression in lead II, III and a VF. Others thought it was just peaked T waves so I called the hospital and declared a STEMI and activated the cath lab. I told Tay, the TOD, that I would rather take the heat for calling a STEMI than for missing one. The physician thought I was wrong at first, but after getting another 12-lead, he agreed and the patient went up to the cath lab. On the way out, Deneen, the Charge Nurse, and Leslie, the PFC, stopped me and told me I had done a good job. I was pleased they went out of their way to tell me, "Good job."

It's been a very busy tour with 17 calls and drills on both days. I'm thankful I'm able to make it through a tour and to also do a good job for both my colleagues and my patients. We should all be thankful today and every day. Thank you Lord. "Always give thanks for all things in the name of our Lord." Ephesians 5:20. Be happy and thankful, showing love and charity, giving to those in need, and practicing kindness and forgiveness.

MAY 6, 2017
Saturday

WE'VE HAD A LOT OF CALLS today but I still managed to take some time to check off a large supply order and get the EMS room properly restocked. Now all my charts are completed and sent to the hospital.

I was at Sport Clips yesterday to get my hair cut where Tracey, the Manager, did an excellent job. She had just returned from Las Vegas where she attended the Sport Clips conference and she was motivated and jazzed about the experience. As I sat there, she told me about how the speakers urged them to reach out, do more, to reach beyond oneself, and to commit to excellence in everything they do.

Today I got to see the last few minutes of the movie *Goonies* which was filmed in Astoria, Oregon, and I was moved by the subtle message. The entire group learned to overcome their obstacles, to have courage, and Sloth taught them to have unconditional love.

These are both great messages for us all to hear: to reach beyond ourselves, to overcome our obstacles, to have courage, and to have unconditional love for all people. We are all to show charity, to give, forgive, and to believe in each other.

I've been thinking a lot about these entries I've been writing. Will anyone care about what I'm writing? I'm just sharing what we all know to be true. We all have struggles, stories, questions, and we usually don't have any real answers. My own struggles have included birth defects, multiple surgeries, a near drowning as a five year old in the river, the loss of my mother, dad, brother, and son, and so many others. You, I am sure, have struggled as well. Who cares about my frailties? I'm not sure anyone really does care, yet I hope that by reading about my frailties, you'll find hope among them. We are all fragile, life is fragile, and maybe it helps to know others are having similar challenges.

I recently experienced a flashback of being beat up when I was in the first grade. At that age, I was an unwell child. Sick with asthma after the near drowning and weak from the recovery from multiple surgeries, I had an assigned bodyguard after being hurt by a bully on the playground. By the end of the school year, I had missed 69% of class so the sisters at the Catholic parochial school thought I should try first grade again after hopefully growing stronger during the summer break. Looking back, it was a good decision. I clearly remember walking home from school that last day of school and being told by a third grader that I was stupid, ugly, and a cripple. The sun was out and shining brightly as I stood on the sidewalk directly across from the White Corner Store feeling like nothing. Maybe all those surgeries and ensuing struggles have made me more compassionate for other people's troubles and situations. Perhaps that is why I've always believed in having strength and courage, why I seem so resilient in the face of personal tragedies and the tragedies I encounter as a paramedic. Maybe you'll be able to get through your skirmishes in life a little easier because I've shared my heartbreaks with you. I hope so. May God bless us all.

> *Rejoice in the Lord always... The Lord is close by, be anxious for nothing, but in everything by prayer and petition with thanksgiving let your requests be made known to God. And the peace of God, which surpasses all comprehension, shall guard your hearts and your minds in Christ Jesus.*
>
> *Philippians 4:4-7*

I'm tired, I am weak, I am worn, take my hand precious Lord, lead me home. I may have one ear, a crooked smile, an asymmetrical face, and a squinty eye but thank the Lord I've not lost my compassion for people. I am so very thankful that MCFD#1 allows me to do what I do best: taking care of people. And I usually do a pretty good job of it. It's a team effort, but thank God I'm still good at caring for the sick and injured.

THIS MORNING CAPTAIN JUAN DELEON WAS giving me such a difficult time. He and Bret just love to give me a ribbing; I suppose they know I can take it, don't find offense, and I'm assuming they do so because they actually like me and respect my medicine. This morning he was being funny while telling stories about medics, nurses, and his wife, who is an awesome nurse in Corvallis. He then says to me, "Well, she likes you! She says you are a good medic! They all say that about you at the hospital." He then added, "I've got to go before you get a big head over it!" I laughed as he headed home. It's nice to know they do respect my hard work and my medicine.

IT'S GETTING LATE NOW AND WE just got back from a call for a rapid heart rate patient. She was fine, just anxious over quitting smoking cold turkey. She had a very nice husband and a worried son though she did just fine.

I'm listening to songs by Angela Primm, especially her Gaither songs. She is such an amazing singer and I find her voice to be inspiring. I especially love to listen to "Take My Hand, Precious Lord" which she sings with Marshall Hall and Jason Crabb on Tent Revival. (You Tube: GaitherVEVO)

MAY 7, 2017
Sunday

I ACCOMPLISHED LOTS OF DIFFERENT TASKS today: double checking the EMS room along with changing a few more things to make it user friendly for the medics, then I drove the recycling box over to the building with a forklift along with James and Bill and we were able to get all the empty boxes flattened and in the container. There were so many boxes that we filled the container. After that, we ran a bunch of calls, had a team lunch, and then had a wildland fire drill.

The day has not been without memories of a year ago when I sat with my mother and held her hand as she died at the Benedictine Center after 18 months of caring for her. Our routine was to get her up in the morning, make her breakfast and get her morning medications, then clean up, make her bed, and visit for a while. We then came back to make her lunch as we visited. Sometimes when it was nice outside, we would go for a car ride or sit outside then come back for dinner and spend the evening with her watching her choice of shows. It was very interesting watching them with her—we would watch *Fox News,* house remodel shows, *Naked and Afraid,* and a freedom show I actually liked. It was about people living in the wilderness while making a go of it the best they could. It's not unlike the rest of us trying to do the best we can with our creature comforts. We would then help her take her night medications and wait until she was ready to go to bed. That was the funny part: we would be dead tired and

December 25, 2012

*"Mayor, Councilwoman, Visionary,
Dedicated Community Servant"*

she would just keep watching more shows. Finally, I would tell her that we should all get some sleep and she would look at us and say, "Oh, are you tired?" Lynell did most of the heavy lifting. She never left Mount Angel for almost two years; one of us would always be there as we made sure to never leave town at the same time. It's now been a year. Good night Mom.

MAY 8, 2017
Monday
IT'S 4:57 IN THE MORNING AND we just returned from a call for a mixed-up boy with a stepdad who has no use for his stepson, and the sad boy knows it. His mom needs to do something; I don't know what but she needs to step in and show her love for her son. We treated him, then took him in to be checked for a couple of issues.

I am fortunate my two boys, Victor 3 and Paul, grew up strong, happy, and successful. Victor 3 was my giver and Army Captain and Paul is my athlete and engineer. They both looked out for each other, coached teams, and always looked out for other people including their mom and dad. I am so lucky to have two great boys.

Why do we press onward? Why do we all keep going? What is the use of trying, living, believing, helping others, and caring for the oppressed? I think we do this to have a goal and purpose in life though the purpose is not always evident to us. For me, my purpose is working at MCFD#1, to take joy in caring for people here in the community, and working with an awesome bunch of people. My colleagues, no matter how much good-natured ribbing they give me, are fantastic people, medics, and firefighters. They may ask me where my walker is and laugh at my gigantic vitamin box but they support my efforts on every call and give me their utmost respect for my medical knowledge and experience. This morning my chaplain skills were also used while talking with the young boy. He needed compassion and understanding and my colleagues, knowing this,

Paul Hoffer

Victor Hoffer 3

stood back ready to jump in but letting me handle the situation through calm and reassuring talk with the boy.

No matter what happens, we have to go forward and have faith in God's timetable while letting go of our own. I would like God to get on *my* timetable because my train schedule has more trains and they run a lot faster than His trains. I was so sad in 2015 when I wasn't picked up by the new ambulance company. But through it all and on God's timetable, I am here with these awesome colleagues, great Battalion Chiefs, and two tremendous leaders in Fire Chief Terry Riley and Deputy Fire Chief Kyle McMann. It was a slow train and a long wait at the train station, but I am here now.

> *Through it all we must all face tomorrow…*
> *We can face uncertain days, because He lives*
> *Because He lives, I can face tomorrow*
> *Because He lives, all fear is gone*
> *Because I know He holds the future and life is worth the living*
> *just because He lives.*
>
> *By Andraé Crouch*

MAY 10, 2017
Wednesday

TODAY I'M WORKING AT THE CLEAR Lake Station, Medic 33, with Chase Redman as my partner. He's a great medic.

I may soon be working down here all the time as I was told this morning that Medic 33 is going to become a day car (an ambulance only in operation during the day). Four medics will have to staff it and I hope I won't be one of them as I know I'll end up being the only single medic while everyone else is promoted to firefighter. It will then just be me with a constantly changing staff. If I am here, it will also make my supply work more difficult to complete and maintain. I hope I can somehow remain at Station 1 and work 48 hour shifts while getting my project duties done more efficiently. Even after all this time, it's still disappointing to walk in at the beginning of a shift and get hit in the face with radical changes. I really do not see the great benefit of having two fewer employees as it reduces coverage and brings in less transport revenue.

Salem Fire responded to a fire in our ambulance district and we responded as the medic team since we were closer than Medic 32. As soon as we arrived, my partner Chase and I immediately hopped out and put our turnouts on to fight the fire. Chase pulled the preload off of Engine 8 while I went to find the occupants of the home to make sure they were safe and out of the inferno. I then helped a

Deputy Fire Chief Kyle McMann, me, and Fire Chief Terry Riley

neighbor get out of his house until the fire was out and made sure all the people in the adjoining homes were safe from fire extension. Then I started walking around handing out bottles of water to everyone as they exited their homes. We were there for a couple of hours until overhaul was complete. We then headed back to the station to clean ourselves up and wash our turnouts.

MAY 11, 2017
Thursday

I HAVE TALKED ABOUT SHOWING COMPASSION to others and I just wanted to share this today:

Be wise in the way you act toward outsiders; make the most of every opportunity. Let your conversation be always full of grace, seasoned with salt, so that you may know how to answer.

Colossians 4:5-6

Be kind and compassionate to one another, tender-hearted, forgiving each other, just as God in Christ also has forgiven you

Ephesians 4:32

I was talking to someone today about my passion for the job. I advised them that if they ever lose their passion, they should find something else to do. Whether you are a firefighter, paramedic, doctor, lawyer, nurse, or anything else, if you don't have passion for what you do and you cannot give it 100%, then retire from that job and find something you *are* passionate about.

Don't compromise your values but always maintain honor, courage, and commitment. Firefighters and medics must show compassion without judgment every day.

May 13, 2017
Saturday

We've had a lot of calls over the last two days of this tour. On Friday, we had drill and it's taken me the whole tour to complete my orders for the EMS supplies as I've only been able to work on them between calls. I've just now finished the accounting documents I produce to keep track of costs and budget line items.

I've recently heard a lot more talk about the new system MCFD#1 is going to implement soon and I have found it to be aggravating. I remind myself to stop being aggravated, to not worry, and that however things fall, I will adapt and overcome. Everything will work out for me and the District and I'll maintain my commitment to excellence and my compassion for my patients. I will be strong, flexible, and committed. With courage, everything will work out for the best. I must be strong and not let other people upset my ability to adapt and subvert my passion and love for what I do each day.

I saw Nathan, an RN, at the hospital last night. He asked me how I was and I

Nathan, RN, and me

told him I was a little discouraged. He hugged me and replied that he was always my friend and is always here for me. He is a great nurse and is teaching new paramedic students at night.

I saw Nancy Bee this morning. When I called the hospital, "Salem Hospital, Medic 31 calling," she answered, "Go ahead Paramedic Hoffer." She recognized my voice. That was rather fun and appreciated at the same time. I so appreciate the staff there; they are so good and kind to me. Thank you SHED.

MAY 14, 2017
Sunday

IT'S MOTHER'S DAY TODAY. HAPPY MOTHER'S Day to everyone.

Today we had a gunshot victim who had been shot in the leg. When we arrived, we found him down on the floor with blood everywhere we looked. A tourniquet was placed on his leg and we started two IVs to infuse 500 ml of fluid during our transport to the hospital. We had a nine minute scene time and a six minute transport time. Except for the tourniquet, all procedures were completed during transport. When the physician took off the tourniquet at the hospital, the blood just poured out of the person's leg and he went to surgery right away. In just a short amount of time, we did a pretty good job.

I mopped the kitchen tonight, emptied the garbage and put the clean dishes away.

We made it through the tour together and took care of a lot of people. Sometimes we save a life and sometimes, as with the last patient tonight, we simply show compassion and understanding for the person's situation by holding their hand and being there for the person in their storm. It feels good to almost be done. Remember 1 Corinthians 13: "So faith, hope, love abide, these three; but the greatest of these is love."

I still have not been to sleep. We just got back from the hospital and I've finished my chart. I gave my report to the nurse, Marie, and she gave me chocolate! The chocolate and her thoughtfulness brighten my spirits. We chatted for a few minutes and I found out that both of her parents have passed away. Her story touched my heart and so I showed her a picture of Victor 3 that I carry in my pocket. She then hugged me and off we went to our duties. She's raised my view of life and how fortunate we all are, even after going through tough times. Thanks Marie.

I have been listening to one of my favorite songs. (GaitherVEVO)

VICTORY IN JESUS
I heard an old, old story,
How a Savior came from glory,
How He gave His life on Calvary
To save a wretch like me;
I heard about His groaning,
Of His precious blood's atoning,
Then I repented of my sins
And won the victory.

Chorus
O victory in Jesus,
My Savior, forever.
He sought me and bought me,
With His redeeming blood;
He loved me ere I knew Him
And all my love is due Him,
He plunged me to victory,
Beneath the cleansing flood.

I heard about His healing,
Of His cleansing pow'r revealing.
How He made the lame to walk again
And caused the blind to see;
And then I cried, "Dear Jesus,
Come and heal my broken spirit,"
And somehow Jesus came and bro't
To me the victory.

I heard about a mansion
He has built for me in glory.
And I heard about the streets of gold
Beyond the crystal sea;
About the angels singing,
And the old redemption story,
And some sweet day I'll sing up there
The song of victory.

Words and Music by E. M. Bartlett
© 1939 - Administered by Integrated Copyright Group, Inc.

MAY 15, 2017
Monday

TODAY HAS BEEN A FUN DAY. First, I got up early and drove to Sherwood where I spoke to the kindergarten class. I've been going up there every year for 14 years to help with their Think First Program that OHSU puts on around the state. In the 1990s, I did their program with a Trailblazer. Now I work independently and go to St. Francis Catholic School to talk to the kindergarteners for an hour about water safety, playground safety, and helmet safety. I tell the kids if they are on wheels, then they need to wear their helmets. It's always a fun time. They all listen and all want to talk so I make it into a game. I tell them, "If you ride a bike wear your…" and they scream out, "Helmet!" We then go outside with a helmet and two cantaloupes to demonstrate the difference a helmet can make. The cantaloupe in the helmet survives intact and the one without it breaks open. The kids just love the demonstration.

Kindergarteners are open to ideas as few others are and as Lynell says, they are honest and pure of heart, seemingly without bias or prejudice, just a bunch of children in a class together. These kids are full of life and energy. They have lots to share and the teacher and I have fun listening to their stories.

I am now at the Convention Center for a marketing meeting. Most people just look at me like I am security, though a few greeted me and were nice to talk with beforehand. I smile the whole time I am walking around with a friendly smile and an open stance. I am the paramedic and am here to help and make you feel better. Two young people, a couple, talked with me and they were so funny. They said I looked like I was 50 and I told them I took vitamins. To this they replied, "Well, the energy that you have makes you seem young." Another person asked directions and admired my name badge holder, the "bling heart." I always try to smile and give positive energy while

providing the best customer service to each individual while meeting their needs whether it's directions, Band-Aids, or ibuprofen; I am here to meet their needs.

Customer service is first in all things and everyone is a customer. Your colleagues at work, your boss, the people you serve at work, and everyone you encounter are customers. For me, it's all about being kind and courteous to everyone. There are plenty of mean people out there being mean for no reason except for the fact they want to spread their unhappiness. So be happy and spread kindness, showing love, charity, and understanding to everyone you encounter every day. Don't be a hater; rather, be the one who is criticized for being kindhearted and considerate.

Forty-one years ago today, I graduated from Southern California College (now Vanguard University of Southern California). Now, 41 years later, I am not a millionaire or even close and I wonder if I am successful. Lynell tells me I've saved many lives, delivered babies, and given comfort to many people. *That is success.* I told you earlier about the Ralph Waldo Emerson saying on the back of Victor's prayer card and I believe it completely. Maybe questioning is what keeps me on the edge to help others and remain strong for the next encounter. A saying a physician once told me was: "You are one complaint from being fired." Well, I *have* been complained about over the years. Each time it was in the mean, evil, and prejudiced mind of the other person and not me. Fortunately, my superiors also know me and realize it is in the other person's mind. I have encountered thousands, more accurately, a hundred thousand plus people over the years. Sometimes you encounter someone having a bad day and they want to pass it on to others. So please be kind. Yes, that is an ongoing theme I have, isn't it? Forty-one years later I hope and believe that I have made a difference in people's lives through a smile, a comforting word, holding a hand, understanding rather than judging, and on occasion, saving a life while reassuring those whose hearts are breaking. To those who are afraid of what is happening to them, I strive to provide comfort, peace, and hope.

SUCCESS

To laugh often and much;
to win the respect of intelligent people and
the affection of honest critics and
endure the betrayal of false friends;
to appreciate beauty, to find the best in others;
to leave the world a bit better;
whether by a healthy child,
a garden patch or a redeemed social condition
to know even one life has breathed easier because you have lived.
This is to have succeeded.

Ralph Waldo Emerson

A few people have said they a want a copy of this star date log I'm writing but I don't think anyone will be interested. It is just ramblings of joy and sadness and hope. This stuff is not exciting like blood and guts, just my struggles, and my search for peace.

MAY 19, 2017
Friday

WHAT A BUSY TWO DAYS I have had in Mt. Angel and here at County! There was a fire in Mt. Angel at 1:00 in the morning to which I responded in the rescue. It was a barn that was fully engulfed with fire. The barn held 600 tons of hay and the team had to put thousands and thousands of gallons of water on it to stop the fire from advancing to the rest of the property and the milk cows who were watching their hay burn. We saved some expensive farm and dairy equipment, lost some other equipment that was at the center of the fire, and sprayed lots of water on the hay. I assisted Command with the fire passports, got Rehab going, and acted as Safety Officer. I was finally released at 4:30 a.m. so I could go to work at MCFD#1. The volunteer firefighters from Mt. Angel, Silverton, Monitor,

The roof had collapsed prior to our arrival.

Bill and Aaron

Cows looking on with red lights flashing around them

and Woodburn Fire did an awesome job; Andy Otte was terrific as Command.

The last two days here have been hectic with lots of work to do around the station between calls and drill. We drilled both Thursday and Friday on wildland fires. I was there yesterday for most of the drill after I had finished up my paperwork and today I stayed back and got a large EMS supply order checked in and the EMS room organized. In between, we ran a bunch of calls. One of our calls was for a combative person on drugs. We also had a fall, a diabetic, a chest pain, swollen legs, and a shortness of breath call.

Last night we had calls at 1:27, 3:01, 4:16, and 5:38 a.m., so we are especially tired this afternoon. We did not go back to sleep when we returned from the last early morning call but caught up on charts and paperwork.

This quote reminds me of how God gives me strength: "The Lord your God is with you, the Mighty Warrior who saves. He will take great delight in you…and will rejoice over you with singing." Zephaniah 3:17. In all we do and with all our burdens, He is with us. Everyone has burdens we don't know about, that is why we need to be kind and thoughtful to everyone. We can gain strength, have hope and faith knowing that the Lord God is with us in the midst of turmoil. Please go and help someone today.

MAY 21, 2017
Sunday

I AM AT THE OREGON CONVENTION Center today for the Python Conference which I find to be very interesting. Python is a language for computers so there are hundreds of computer program developers listening to talks. It's fun.

Earlier in my shift, I walked out to the loading dock where I saw Barbara riding on a standing cart. We waved at each other before she drove over and jumped off her cart to give me a hug. She told me that whenever she sees me, she feels happy and blessed. Well, I feel happy and blessed that she would stop and say hello to me and then say such kind words. She has a difficult job cleaning up after everyone, moving chairs and tables, and setting up and taking down everything before and after an event. She is awesome. Thanks Barbara.

I listened to some TEDx talks on the drive up this morning about finding one's purpose in life. To sum up all those talks I listened to, I would say we should focus on the people we serve and strive to make other people happy, making sure they're well taken care of and secure in life. The second TEDx talk I listened to suggested that one should do what's valuable for society, to focus on becoming good at something which genuinely helps others and makes the world a better place. That's the secret to a fulfilling career—helping others.

I am pretty sure this is why I do what I do in life. As an attorney, I help people a little at a time but what I do best is take care of people as a paramedic. I really don't know what else to do but take care of people in their moment of need. When people are having a crisis, I get to be there and help them through their crisis. Maybe I stop the bleeding, ease the shortness of breath, treat the chest pain, deliver a baby, or just provide comfort and reassurance to a person. Maybe the Grandma just lost her husband and needs some kindness. That is what I do best.

I have started plenty of intravenous lines in the field, maybe 70,999 (plus), and treated lots of people with albuterol and oxygen, but my greatest skill is when I'm able to recognize fear and confusion in the patient and I get to step in, kneel down next to the recliner, and give direction, comfort, and reassurance. For example, think of a married couple who have been married for many years. They are sitting in their chairs and one doesn't feel right. That person turns to their spouse and says, "Dad, I don't feel good. What should I do?" Dad says, "Well Mom, I think you should go to the hospital and get checked out." She replies, "Okay, that's what I will do." Years later, Dad dies and she is sitting there feeling unwell; she no longer has anyone to ask for advice or direction. She calls 911 and when the medics arrive, she is looking to us for a professional medical opinion of what she should do because she feels sick. Some medics say to her, "We can't make you go to the hospital so it's totally up to you." That doesn't help her; she is looking for direction since Dad is gone. I like to kneel down and give her a professional medical opinion. "Well, Mrs. Jones, I think you should go in and get checked out by a physician at the hospital." "Really?" she says. "Yes," I say, "if you were my mom, I would want you to get checked out." I can then see relief in her face as she tells me she'll go in and get checked out. The same scenario is true when Dad has lost his wife and is totally lost without her. "Well, sir, I am pretty sure your wife would have wanted you to go in and be seen today. She would want you to be checked out by a doctor." He goes, "Okay, let's go."

I have started a lot of intravenous lines in a moving ambulance, bouncing down the road to the hospital but what I do best is to give comfort and reassurance. I show respect and courtesy, and I treat patients like they are my own family. I am fulfilling my purpose in life: to be a helper. My life has meaning as I strive to make the world, my neighborhood, and my community a better place.

Altruism is the belief in and practice of selfless concern for the well-being of others and being altruistic is a good thing to become. I urge you to have a purpose in your life and to be valuable to your community. Help the poor, the destitute, and the disenfranchised, and seek out those who may be suffering in silence.

May 24, 2017
Wednesday

I AM EXTREMELY SICK TODAY. LAST night I ate too late and then regurgitated it all when I fell asleep. Between the hot and cold flashes along with the severe pain all over my body, I wanted to call in sick but couldn't since it was 3 in the morning. Now I'm at the station and I continue to have a headache and chills while feeling hot and every once in a while, I can't breathe. I used an old inhaler I had in my bag and took some antihistamine along with ibuprofen. Now I just hurt everywhere.

We just returned from a call for a sick person though I, too, feel awful. I'm now going to finish their chart and go rest.

May 25, 2017
Thursday

WE WERE SO BUSY LAST NIGHT with all kinds of calls for sick people who needed help from us. One remarkable call came in just before midnight for a person not breathing. While we were driving to their location, the call was changed to a CPR call and when we arrived, we found two women doing CPR on a man on top of a flatbed trailer in the garage! Though no one wanted to tell us exactly what was going on, we stopped CPR and found a pulse but he wasn't breathing! I jabbed him with two milligrams of Narcan IM in his upper arm and in just a few seconds, he started breathing and in 30 seconds, he was talking to us. He told me he had snorted OxyContin and we took him to the hospital for an evaluation to make sure there was nothing else going on with him. From dead to alive, that's always a nice outcome.

This morning we got blasted with calls. Two of them were for people very sick with the flu. My understanding is that the flu or something similar is going around the state. Then I got all the supplies that came in checked off and the supply room stocked for the next few days.

At the hospital, they are always kind and considerate to me. This morning one nurse could tell I looked a little haggard, patted me on the back, and just smiled. While giving a turnover report tonight, Stephanie, the charge nurse, came over and greeted me. I told her I looked like a mess to which she laughed and told me I looked fine. I really do look awful, though, after two days of work and not feeling well. My friends at Salem Hospital Emergency Department are amazing. With all the stress they deal with due to the enormous amount of patients seen there every hour of every day, they are still smiling. Listening to my turnover reports, they still find space to appreciate what we do in the pre-hospital setting.

Tonight, say a prayer for all the nurses, techs, housekeepers, and doctors who are working in emergency departments around the world. It is not an easy job.

MAY 27, 2017
Saturday

I AM WORKING TODAY AT STATION 2, Medic 32, for a short 12 hour shift to help someone else so he can take the day off with his family. We have already run one call for a man who was found in the grass asleep. When the engine arrived, he immediately told them he wanted to go to the hospital so they called us and we took him in.

I have an intern paramedic student with me today. He is Iwaniw's intern from Chemeketa Community College. I have been able to work with a number of fire students but not any paramedic students. We are going to go over things throughout the day including how to start intravenous lines and assessing someone's condition among whatever else comes up. I will also make sure they know my three main rules:

1. Never make your partner look bad
2. If you think the patient needs an intravenous line, they need an intravenous line
3. If you think it's a trauma entry, it's a trauma entry

There are more rules, but that's a start.

Monday is Memorial Day and the Mt. Angel Fire District will be helping with a service at the cemetery. Though the service has been canceled the last few years due to rain, this year we are supposed to have great weather and will be able to walk from the American Legion Hall in a procession to the cemetery and then hold a remembrance service. I always look forward to this day and am glad we finally get to do it.

Knowing I would be working today, last Friday I put out flowers, flags, and lights along with some glitter on the graves of my family including Dad, the Fire Chief; Mom, the Mayor; my brother John, who served in the Air Force; and my son, Victor 3, who was in the Army. Each of them served their community in many ways and all built programs that continue today. They knew what it was to give

Victor 3. Victor was a fine young man. He looked out for others first and then himself.

Fire Chief Victor Hoffer; Mayor Margaret Hoffer; SGT John Victor Hoffer, US Air Force; and Captain Victor Jeremiah Hoffer, US Army

unselfish service to others and were the perfect embodiment of what altruism means: the belief in and practice of disinterested and selfless concern for the well-being of others.

On Memorial Day we should all be thankful for the men and women who protect our beautiful country and our nation. We should acknowledge their service and honor those who have fallen, along with being thankful to those who guard our nation today. God Bless America and the freedom and liberty we hold so dear in our hearts.

Just as we honor others, we must also be willing to give of ourselves by making sacrifices and helping our communities. I am thankful for all the staff at Salem Hospital Emergency. Thank you for all you do. Let's also acknowledge the men and women who protect us daily: EMTs, paramedics, and firefighters. These men and women serve our communities every day and they all serve our nation by keeping us safe.

We were at the hospital earlier today when I saw a friend from another company. He told his trainee that his first day 26 years ago was with me when I tossed him the keys and said, "Let's go!" He

Larry Hornaday and me

remembers better than I do that the call was for a car which had run into a tree and the older woman behind the wheel was severely injured. As she was a trauma entry, we went code 3 with red lights and sirens to the hospital. He reminded me that driving her in was the first time he had ever driven code 3. Twenty-six years later, he is still out there taking care of people. I asked him to please take my greetings to my friends still working at the company. He is a solid and kind man and I am glad to have worked with him.

I want to share some quotes that have been on my heart:

Our greatest weakness lies in giving up. The most certain way to succeed is always to try just one more time.

Thomas A. Edison

The will to win, the desire to succeed, the urge to reach your full potential…these are the keys that will unlock the door to personal excellence.

Confucius

Every man must decide whether he will walk in the light of creative altruism or in the darkness of destructive selfishness.

Martin Luther King, Jr.

Always desire to learn something useful.

Sophocles

Smile, keep trying, be strong, have faith, show compassion, love, and charity, lead by being the servant-leader, measure your success by your kindness to others, help others, and give freely. Give to the widows and the poor, never give up, smile.

Me

MAY 28, 2017
Sunday

I'M AT THE ARLENE SCHNITZER CONCERT Hall tonight doing medical standby. I haven't been down to the ASCH for a while and it's nice to see all the ushers again. They're such a pleasure to talk with before the show. Tonight is Rodriguez with Arum Raet as the opening act. Several friends are also working tonight: Rick, who also supervises at the Convention Center, is at the stage door; Ed, one of my favorite ushers, is here tonight taking tickets on the Park side of the building; and Rebecca, the House Manager, always helps me out.

Ed and me

Just now an usher spotted a person who was videotaping. You can't do that at a show without permission! The man said he was family but the chief usher instructed him to get a photo pass, which is the correct answer. He handled it perfectly.

I spoke with a couple from Austin, Texas, who are here in Portland for the concert. They were wonderful people; I should have gotten their first names. To the couple: you will never read this, but thank you for the enjoyable conversation.

MAY 29, 2017
Monday – Memorial Day

MAY 31, 2017
Wednesday

LAST WEEK, A DOCTOR REMOVED A suspicious area from my skin. The biopsy came back from that and they told me they need to remove the remainder of the growth which they did today. I now have a four inch incision on my chest. Today's biopsy will be back next week.

JUNE

JUNE 1, 2017
Saturday

June 2, 2017
Friday

I ATTENDED THE GOVERNOR'S ADVISORY COMMITTEE on DUII this morning along with Shirley Wise from NHTSA Region 10. Shirley told me I ought to apply for the National EMS Advisory Committee within NHTSA. I was honored she thought I should apply though I don't think I have the political juice to be appointed. Still, I'm going to turn in an application and see what happens. Thank you, Shirley, for your belief in me.

This afternoon we responded to a call for a garage fire that was threatening the main structure of the house. Mt. Angel Fire got out there and did a terrific job of putting out the fire before it spread to the house. I came out in the rescue to pass out water and then clean up the empty bottles. The person who spotted the fire is actually Gary Raid, our Fire District Treasurer, so I walked down to his house to get his information. I really like Gary and knew his dad Charlie. Charlie and I used to chat at the post office in the mornings and Gary played football for the Green Bay Packers under Coach Vince Lombardi. Very cool!

Gary Raid and me

JUNE 3, 2017
Saturday

THERE WAS A FIRE IN MONITOR today which was so big that Monitor, Mt. Angel, Woodburn, Silverton, Hubbard, and Molalla fire departments all responded. I went out on Engine 465 to set up a rehab area then Air 21 arrived to set up a second. Pray for all first responders and for their safety.

MAFD: Zach, Dean, Ryan, Ron, Chris

Fire Chief Paul Iverson and Fire Chief Jim Trierweiler

June 4, 2017
Sunday

I have been asking for the Lord's help to figure out how to keep my star date log of this probie year meaningful, uplifting, and inspiring. Though I really don't know the answer of how someone reading this would find something useful for their lives, I trust God that there is something for everyone. For myself, the scripture and quotes are helpful, but what is here for everyone else?

I was talking recently with a colleague about how one of the employees she manages was rude to another. There is no reason to be rude and obnoxious. She solved the immediate issue right away by holding the employee accountable for their rudeness and making it clear that such behavior was unacceptable. My colleagues and I have been treated rudely ourselves and our conclusion is that simple courtesy is always appropriate.

Remember, just like children who get away with bad behavior, adults who are not held accountable will continue their bad behavior. We are not always in the position to hold others accountable so I would say the most important person to hold accountable is oneself. Please be courteous and polite, think of others' feelings, and be strong.

> *God is loving and good; he will remember the help and the love you show to his children and the support, comfort, and charity you continue to show every day.*
>
> *Hebrews 6:10*

June 6, 2017
Tuesday

We had a transformer fire yesterday morning that was a major power source to the college. Housed in a large cabinet 6 feet by 6 feet in size, it was smoking when we first arrived. Then a fire exploded from the box. The electric company soon arrived at the scene and a worker disengaged the electrical supply from the box before opening the cabinet doors. This introduced oxygen to the box so there was another explosion of electricity along with more flames. The worker opening the door could have been killed but he wasn't even injured! The blast was amazing.

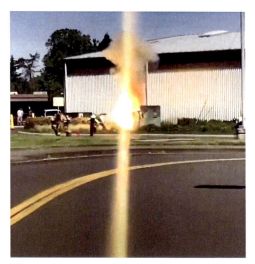

Everyone is running away from the blast!

My partner talked to the Fire Chief this afternoon and was told he's getting a promotion and moving shifts. For myself, I trust the Fire Chief and the Deputy Fire Chief that they will come through for me as well after the changes are instituted in July.

We drove by the house of the first client I had as an attorney. She was Italian and would have me over for lunch every few months. I probably ate more vegetables at her house than I ever had before. I would look at her with a look that plainly said, "Really? You want me to eat something green, or red, or yellow?" She would simply smile and tell me how good they were for me. We always had very pleasant conversations as I worked on her will and I enjoyed hearing her stories from her past.

When I was first working on her will, she told me she had a son in Salem but that they never spoke to each other and thus she left him out of any inheritance. I wrote it just as she requested but after she signed the will, I told her how fortunate she was to have a son and that she should go to him to talk with him and try to reconcile. She did just that and they were both very happy as a result! With that reconciliation in their relationship along with some forgiveness, they were able to share peace and happiness and have the bond between mother and son restored. I joyfully wrote her a new will without charge.

A little forgiveness with the goal of reconciliation would likely bring us all peace and happiness. Oscar Wilde said "Children begin by loving their parents; after a time they judge them; rarely, if ever, do they forgive them." This being said, we should all reach out to forgive and love our children and children should all reach out to forgive and love their parents. The unfortunate thing about life is that people are misunderstood and their reasons for what they sometimes do are misunderstood by others. We should all seek peace with our friends and family. Yes, this is not always possible, but where peace and love can be found, we should do our best to plant the seeds of harmony and reconciliation.

June 7, 2017
Wednesday

We had a group of second graders at the Mt. Angel Fire Station for public education. We taught them "Stop, Drop, and Roll," gave E.D.I.T.H. reminders for the parents, toured Engine 455, and the kids sprayed water with me while I was in charge of the deck gun.

June 8, 2017
Thursday

The Speed Zone Review Panel met today and I am on the committee as the Chair of the OTSC. After an engineering review and public hearings throughout the state, we met to decide if we wanted to change the speed for trucks on Interstate highways in Oregon. After a lengthy discussion, we decided to recommend to the Oregon Transportation Commission to increase truck speeds and reduce the differential between the speeds of cars and trucks. The OTC will officially be the group that changes the Oregon Administrative Rule.

June 9, 2017
Friday

Today I just got to be in my home town of Mt Angel and I was so happy.

June 10, 2017
Saturday – Portland Rose Parade

I worked at the Oregon Convention Center today on medical standby. The Convention Center has an ADA area along with a medic available for the crowd. This is the second year I got to run medical and it was great to be there. I spoke to a number of the horseback riders and after the parade I helped the event managers pick up chairs and garbage and roll up the orange netting.

As I was preparing to go into the Convention Center, I was watching

Miss Vancouver Rodeo

people getting the horses ready for the parade. The parents were helping along with the coaches who were putting flowers on the horses. Well, one of the horses did its business on the street and the father of the Clark County Rodeo Princess went over with a shovel and broom to clean it up. I was impressed he did that and it showed me how much he loves his daughter. It was touching to see the love of a father for his child.

Reser's float dancer

Mayor Ted Wheeler and me

June 12, 2017
Monday

THE PAST TWO DAYS HAVE BEEN extremely busy with calls and frustration. I keep telling myself not to be frustrated, that I must trust and believe things will work themselves out here at County. I know that it's my choice to be frustrated, that I let the promotions talk discourage me when there is no talk of any promotion for me. The union did tell me they'll work on negotiating my pay in 2018 though they are also taking $102 out of my paycheck every month. I should not and must not be frustrated. It is silly and ridiculous to worry. I hereby stop!

At 2:30 this morning we had a call for a woman who was gasping for breath. She has COPD and was not able to move any air when attempting to breathe. We quickly loaded her into the ambulance and in the brief moments of transport, made her feel better. I started an intravenous line, put CPAP on her, and gave her a breathing treatment, and then a dose of Dexamethasone. I was happy we were able to accomplish so much for her in so short a time.

This morning we had two calls for people with chest pain and another call for someone who fell and broke a hip. Just as with medics

Eli, Bret, me, and Captain Kettering

all over the world, we were able to help our patients and deliver them quickly to the hospital.

Bret, the engineer paramedic on Engine 315, is here today. He's a great medic and helped me a lot with a patient we transported to the hospital earlier today.

♦♦♦

I'VE JUST FINISHED WORKING ON RESTOCKING the EMS room. There should be enough supplies set out for the next few days though I will need to order more supplies during the next tour to keep up with demand. I enjoy ordering and restocking supplies as the ongoing project lets me come up with ways to make it better and easier for the crews when they come in to restock their medics.

This has been a good tour and my frustration seems trivial now. We've had some great calls where we were able to do well by our patients and see positive outcomes. Such results are exactly what I want from a shift— taking care of people with good outcomes for them.

Bret showed me his Facebook page earlier. I don't have a Facebook account so I asked him to look up Paul's page so I could see it. There were pictures of him running along with a scripture verse. It was 1 Corinthians 13:7: "Love always protects, always trusts, always hopes, always perseveres." You can also interpret it as "Love never stops being patient, never stops believing, never stops hoping, never gives up," or "Love bears all things, believes all things, hopes all things, endures all things."

I have a smart son. Already he's figured out that love and patience are the keys to life. I am reminded to do the same. Go out showing kindness and try to understand people's struggles as well as having patience with your own. Persevere and be resilient.

JUNE 13, 2017
Tuesday

WHEN I LEFT WORK THIS MORNING, I went directly to go lead the Oregon Transportation Safety Committee meeting. We voted to approve several items and the items needing conversation were robustly discussed. It was, overall, a very successful meeting. The Transportation Safety Division Administrator, Troy Costales, from ODOT told me I did a good job today. Thanks Troy.

Over these last few months, I have been downtrodden at times, felt discouraged and frustrated, and happy as well. Today I just want to remember Psalm 91 and say: "The Lord is my refuge and my fortress, my God, in whom I trust."

Me as the Chair for the Oregon Transportation Safety Committee, Governor Victor G. Atiyeh Board Room, Department of Public Safety Standards and Training

June 16, 2017
Friday

I spent yesterday at the Oregon Transportation Commission meeting where we discussed how marijuana impairs people's ability to drive and the 163% dramatic increase in crashes Colorado has experienced since marijuana was legalized in 2014. In the afternoon, the Highway Safety Performance Plan was presented for approval. By the time I came out,  I saw my parking pass had been incorrectly filled out and that I had received a $50 parking ticket even though I had placed my incorrect pass in the window. That was frustrating.

After the meeting, I then attended the Governor's Advisory Committee on Motorcycle Safety. Tonight we talked about motorcyclists carrying tourniquets in a medical pack as there was a major incident recently where tourniquets may have saved lives. I talked to Jeff, the program manager for motorcycle safety, and suggested to him we put together a 15 minute talk to be given at motorcycle rallies about tourniquets and then handing out sets of 2 and an Israeli trauma bandage for everyone who attends. We could start the program in Oregon and then recommend it be expanded nationwide. We could even include a hands-only CPR class. I think this would be an awesome program and provide awareness on how to save lives. I just need to find partners who would be willing to fund the idea and get the program started. I am hopeful.

June 17, 2017
Monday

Saturday was crazy! We left the Station at 7:00 a.m. and finally got a break at 7 p.m. In all, we had seven calls and were constantly clearing one call and taking another. All my charts and restocking are now done and I am sitting down with a snack.

Between all those calls, we had breathing problems, strokes, cuts, sick people, and trauma calls. The trauma call we had was for a 7 year old girl who fell 10 feet out of a treehouse. When we arrived, she was scared and hurt. We immediately applied a C-Collar, a pediatric backboard, started an intravenous line, and I made her a trauma entry. I was particularly worried about her belly as she had lots of pain in her abdomen and with the height of the fall, she absolutely needed to be a trauma entry. I was told later that she will be fine; I was so relieved and happy to hear that news.

I decided to go to bed early so by 8:00 p.m. I was resting in my room. That turned out to be a good idea as we started getting call after call at 11:00 p.m. That first call at 11:00 was for a hostile boy in a foster care home. We talked to him for a long time. It turned out that the state social worker took away his electronic games for the weekend which are his only distraction and so his frustration kept building up to the breaking point. With all due respect, I rarely ever understand why social workers here in Oregon make decisions the way they do. By the time we were done talking with the boy, he felt better and was able to cope. We cared enough about him to help him find resolution, not frustration.

As soon as we finished that call, we took another for a sick person and then our third call for the day was what we call "a trap." A trap is when a vehicle is in a crash and people are trapped inside. We found the vehicle on its side in a ditch with the driver's door facing down. The driver trapped inside was a high school girl and with the rear hatch jammed against the ditch, the girl couldn't climb out and was too scared to do anything but lay there. The rescue team discussed the situation and decided to cut the roof off in order to get her out. After first stabilizing the vehicle, they used the Halmatro extrication tools to cut the car apart so they could get to the girl. They did a terrific job and the girl was uninjured. Nice work!

Our next call was for a person who had taken a huge dose of Valium (Diazepam) as well as several glasses of wine. By the time we arrived, she was unconscious but breathing. Our first task was to get her out of her house which was a difficult task all by itself. By the time we were on the way to the hospital, she started to come around enough to mumble and slur her words though we couldn't understand a word she said to us. I was able to get a 20 gauge intravenous line established as we drove down the highway and we gave her a fluid bolus of Normal Saline since her blood pressure was initially 70/40. I had already given her Narcan IM (intramuscular injection) just in case narcotics were involved. The fluid seemed to help her mental state for by the time we got to the hospital, she was

cussing at me and all the hospital staff. Though she mumbled the rest of her words, all the four letter ones came out crystal clear.

Between all the calls, we have already treated a stroke, a diabetic, and responded to smoke coming from a house. The smoke turned out to be a burn barrel behind the house. While there, I got to see Captain Elmer from Engine 10. They responded to the fire from Salem and he wished me a happy Father's Day and shook my hand. He has always been great to me and shown great courtesy and respect.

I hope to watch some of the College World Series today. First, I'm going to make some lunch and rest for a few minutes. Tomorrow is Father's Day. Happy Father's Day to me.

June 18, 2017
Sunday – Father's Day

When a father gives to his son, both laugh; when a son gives to his father, both cry.

William Shakespeare

THIS QUOTE SPARKED A MEMORY ABOUT my dad. My dad started volunteering with the Mt. Angel Fire Department in 1950 while working as a truck driver. By 1987, he had 37 years in as a volunteer and 15 years in as the Fire Chief so we held a celebration for him. People who attended gave him a lot of nice gifts in appreciation for his dedicated service. Victor 3 and I gave him a special pen set with a holder for his desk. On an attached plate, we had it engraved so he could always remember that day. It said:

Congratulations
to Chief Vic Hoffer on 37 years of service
from your Son Victor Hoffer and
your Grandson Victor Hoffer 3.

He was so surprised to get a gift from us which, I think, is the best way to have a surprise—when a surprise is kept top secret! When he opened our gift, he was so happy and had the biggest smile on his face. He particularly loved the nameplate: "Chief Vic Hoffer." He then turned over the pen set to the other side and read the words we'd engraved. When he looked up at us, he had tears in his eyes. He was so proud of me and Victor 3 and we were so very proud of Grandpa. That was the one and only time I ever saw him with a tear in his eye.

When my father was growing up, the Hoffer family was very poor. After school he worked in the flax plant and gave his paycheck to his mother every week. As an adult, he could see what was inside of people. If a person didn't have a dollar in their pocket for a soda pop, he could tell and would ask them, "Do you want something to drink?" The person would answer no but he pulled out a dollar to pay for it anyway. I watched this happen many times. He looked out for *everyone.* Sometimes he was criticized by those who didn't understand why he was always gathering things for other people and particularly the fire department guys. He never gathered things for himself. He was a lot like the nurse in the TV show *MASH* who never shared her fudge with the other nurses. The other nurses spent a lot of time criticizing her not knowing she shared it all with the wounded. That is how Dad was—he gave to his community and looked out for others despite being criticized by the jealous and the uninformed. My father was a wonderful example of love, generosity, forgiveness, and showing charity. I strive to build those qualities into my own life.

Just like my dad who looked out for me, who protected and helped me, God is here for us and commands His angels to protect you and to be your bodyguards throughout all your days. The angels will have your back and lift you up so that you will not strike your foot and you will not be hurt by others. (Psalm 91)

♦♦♦

IT'S NOW GETTING LATE, 11:06 P.M., and we just got back to the station after answering a lot of calls.

One of the calls we had was for a teenage girl who had a disagreement with her mom. She then took a large amount of pills and immediately regretted doing so. I transported her to the hospital and found her to be a nice person. My heart went out to her—she is struggling and though I don't know what her struggles are, I do know we *all* go through struggles and that we somehow need to find friends to help us get through them. I told her though I don't know what she's going through, I hope she will work things out with her mom. Unfortunately, struggles never stop, they just change. I also asked her to promise me the next time she is frustrated and aggravated that she'll simply take a breath, find some space for herself, and NOT do anything like she did today. She promised me that she would. Being young today is a big enough struggle and then being poor makes life even more difficult. Many people can't see their way out of the deep abyss they find themselves in every day. Pray for her, and when you see her and others like her, give to them your time, your prayers, your help, and your understanding. Withhold your judgment and simply love them. I can't tell you her name so find her in the eyes of those around you and lend to them a sympathetic heart and a compassionate ear. Show the love of God to her.

Another call we responded to was for a sick woman whom we transported to the hospital. On the way there, she told me about her beautiful grandchildren and how their father was in Russia with Youth with a Mission(YWAM). I replied to her I knew YWAM and her eyes opened up wide in surprise. It turns out her husband attended the same college I did, Southern California College, now Vanguard University. She also told me she knew the Reverend Doctor George O. Wood and that she was familiar with the church where I was the Senior Minister Intern, Newport-Mesa Christian Center. I related to her that by the end of the year at Newport-Mesa they called me the "Minister of Helps" as I did all the help type jobs at the church. It is such a small world and was perfect timing for me to be in the correct place to be assigned to her call.

We had a meeting tonight about the scheduling changes and the promotions being handed out to some of my colleagues. I am delighted Eli and Matt are going to get their firefighter promotions but I worry what will happen to me. I know I should simply trust, not worry, have faith, and I'll get there, but right now, I feel like I'm treated as an inferior person and I feel discouraged about it.

Tomorrow I work for St. Paul Fire.

JUNE 19, 2017
Monday

A MOST UNFORTUNATE CALL HAPPENED EARLIER. A woman with multiple medical problems was having breathing problems and by the time we arrived, both her breathing and heart had stopped completely. Eli and I started CPR immediately as well as placing an advanced airway and an IO line. After half an hour, though, we had to pronounce her dead even after doing everything humanly possible to bring her back. I failed.

Though our team was pretty much perfect, nothing could have helped her. Months ago, she had stopped taking her medications as she could no longer afford them. It's a failure of society to not take care of her, a failure of insurance companies and the government. I believe the real reason they charge a copayment is to keep people from using their insurance when seeking medical help. It's okay for the CEOs who have all the insurance and money they need for care as they rake in millions of dollars every year. That is what is really wrong with America: corporate greed. Who cares about the poor as long as the few get their 10 or 20 million dollars each year? How much money is enough money?

I have worked for a workers compensation insurance company as a law clerk; they paid their adjusters bonuses for denials! They try to wear people down until they give up. What a sad thing for America that people are unimportant and money is god. So many children are hungry each day; they don't have shoes and clothes that fit and they live in sad conditions. Even the CEOs who do want to give money away have so many stipulations. Give *me* money to give away and I will show you how people can be helped. There is so much bias and politics in so many giveaways. How about we give out of love, faith, hope, and compassion and have real social justice, not the made up self-serving social justice politicians use to gain more power and money for themselves? We need to serve God's children and not the special foundations which only serve as slush funds for the self-aggrandizement of the rich. We need to show respect and love to others, to give and forgive, to seek to help the widows and the orphans and to not ever expect something in return.

In all you do, please do it without condition. The love of God for his children is unconditional, so, too, should *our* love be unconditional. As my favorite song goes, "Precious Lord take my hand, I am tired, I am weak, I am worn." Practice unconditional love.

June 20, 2017
Tuesday

LAST NIGHT I WAS CALLED AND mandatoried to work today on Medic 32 with Aaron. I was working in St. Paul and came straight from there this morning. Aaron is young and a very good medic and firefighter. It will be a pleasure working with him.

Congress is talking healthcare reform this week and deciding who receives health care through insurance and how much they receive.

There is a lot of controversy around the discussions because the plans are being kept secret from the people of America. The real way to resolve the issue is simple: Congress and all federal workers should have the same insurance coverage as the poorest people of America, the same as Medicare recipients, and the same as our veterans. If U.S. Senators and Representatives had to have the same healthcare as the rest of America, the coverage would be equitable for all people.

I just now received an email that Medicare is once again making rules to hurt the people who are supposed to be helping others. There is now another ambulance rule on mileage in order to reduce payments for transports which will hurt the people they are supposed to help. It's abhorrent, hateful, and repugnant. Congress should have to have the same rules as the rest of America!

> *What good is it for someone to gain the whole world, yet forfeit their soul?*
>
> Mark 8:36

Life is precious and we need to respect *all* people. The woman who died the other day just wanted good health. She just needed medicine and good healthcare to feel better and to live a full happy life. We need to not be so greedy in America.

Outside Station 2 today

Love is the all-important attribute.
Love is patient,
Love is kind,
Love bears all things,
Love believes all things,
Love hopes all things,
Love endures all things.
Love never fails,
There is faith, and hope, and love, all three are important; but
the greater of these is love.

1 Corinthians 13:4-7, 13

It's through love for all of humankind that one serves the world. Don't be arrogant and superior but show courtesy and respect for all people. Don't boast or brag like the Pharisees who showed off their wealth but give quietly, help anonymously, forgive the wrong suffered by you. All of this should be done with love in your heart, not thinking your side is always right and the other side is always wrong, but acting with charity and generosity.

Demagoguery is ridiculous. Stop the stupidity and help the people around you. Politicians should do what is right for the people. A demagogue is evil and hateful. Do you want votes and the approval of your party, who will turn on you tomorrow, or do you want to do what is right for the community? The same is to be said of the CEOs of America. They take jobs away from the community and create devastation and ruin for American families so they can have a bigger bonus. Politicians from all sides should be ashamed and CEOs as well should be ashamed of what they have created. They will always have great insurance for themselves as they take it away from working America. They will never wonder if they will have enough money to feed their children, pay the rent, buy medicine, or pay the electric bill, for they have looked out for their evil selves first, foremost, and last. Their god is power and money.

June 23, 2017
Friday

TODAY HAS BEEN FRUSTRATING SO FAR. Early this morning we got called out to a CPR call. Upon arrival, we found an elderly woman dead in her bed. We cleared that call to go back to a meeting and saw the other medic had a call for which we were closer so we took it over. When we arrived, we found a young man in severe respiratory distress along with chest pain and breathing difficulty. He had been short of breath for a week but it worsened to such an extent that he called for help. We quickly transported him to the hospital with a five minute scene time and a six minute transport time but he got sick as we took him out of the ambulance. It took a minute to get him in and as soon as we moved him to a hospital bed, his breathing stopped so I bagged him and then respiratory took over for me. As I stepped out to give the report, he coded but they got him back and he's in ICU now.

Between the call today, the woman who was dead in her bed this morning, the young woman who died last week, and then my friend who died and who I treated to no avail last week, it seems like too much. Please pray for me.

On our last call, no one would answer the door and we couldn't get in. We were looking for an open window when we got a call from dispatch who told us the person left the scene and no one was home.

Regarding the young man from earlier today, Peter and Chuck stopped me the last time we were at the hospital to tell me

the patient was doing better and that we did a great job. He would be dead without what we did for him.

We have gone to the hospital a few more times tonight. Stacey is the PFC for the evening and is the person I go to when I have a patient who is misbehaving and needs a talking to in order to adjust their behavior. You can always count on her to be there for all the medics and is someone who really gets the job done.

June 24, 2017
Saturday

TODAY SHOULD BE AN INTERESTING AND challenging day. The temperature is supposed to hit 102° and the morning has already been a little busy. All of the medics have transported at least once to the hospital. I have inventoried and stocked the EMS room and placed a supply order.

At the hospital this morning, Doctor Spangle stopped me to tell me that we did a great job on our critical patient yesterday. She said he wouldn't have made it without what we did for him. She said that he was moving around and improving by the time he was sent upstairs to ICU yesterday. I thanked her for her kind words.

> *The Lord will keep you from all harm—he will watch over your life; the Lord will look out for you wherever you go, right now and always.*
>
> *Psalm 121:7-8*

Those are comforting words for all of us.

Though it's extremely hot out there, the calls have been light. So far, I have had a domestic call and another for back pain. The person with back pain was the nicest elderly lady. She must have weighed 90 pounds at most and was simply uncomfortable and lonely. She received "TLC" from us and more from the hospital. Some days I wish we had a system to go visit people who have no one to talk to all day long. She was living in a garage apartment with her dog and I could tell she felt alone and was eager to talk to us and the nurses at the hospital. In the many years I have been doing this, I have always wanted to go visit people and I haven't. It would be a full-time job for anyone.

We could have an entire agency or church or youth group going out and visiting people and it would become a full-time job. There are so many people who need our help. I have talked a lot about helping out with food and clothes and not much about visiting but that is another place where all of us could seek out the lonely. There is so much to do and so little time to do it all. I do not have the answers but I hear their cries for help every day.

June 25, 2017
Sunday

AFTER SEVERAL CALLS THROUGHOUT THE NIGHT, we got back to the station this morning around 5:00 a.m. and I went back to sleep for an hour. Now I am at the Convention Center until 10:00 p.m.

It's been a wonderful day so far. There are three conferences going on all at once: the Islamic Center of Portland, Eid-al-Fitr; Heroes and Villains Fan Fest; and an Evolution Conference. This is freedom at its best—all of these different belief systems, cultures, great diversity in thoughts, opinions, and various points of view all doing what they want to do at the same time. I love it.

I've really enjoyed helping everybody here. First I helped a daughter, mother, and grandmother at the Islamic event when they got turned around and needed a little help. The children were so happy and dressed up.

There were lots of happy faces at the Fan Fest as well. I really enjoyed seeing another group of people free to express themselves

with costumes of various genres. My friend
Ashley was walking around and everyone was
getting photos with her in costume. I went
along with it as well and a photo was taken of
me. After all, I am in a paramedic costume!

At the Evolution Conference, people
are dressed like college kids and are all
talking science. Meetings are happening,
talks are being given, and posters are being
presented. It's amazing to see first-hand the diversity of thought all
in one building with everyone showing respect to one another. This
is what freedom of speech and expression means in a civilized society.
This is America.

I just had a nice talk with Evolution Conference goer, Doctor
Kate L. Hertweck, Ph.D., Assistant Professor of Biology at the
University of Texas in Tyler. Just before I was scheduled to be done
for the day, we talked about science and college students and how
different people learn in various ways. It was a very interesting
discussion.

Today was a joy and reaffirmed my belief that all people should
be treated with respect and courtesy. Working together in peace and
harmony toward a goal of better understanding and appreciation for
all beliefs, opinions, and ideas
through courtesy, respect and
appreciation for all of humankind and reverence for life
makes the world a better place
for all to live and grow. Believe
in good, reject hate.

JUNE 29, 2017
Thursday

GOOD MORNING. I AM WORKING AT Station 1 on Medic 31 today. July 1ˢᵗ is moving day for people as we are reassigned to different stations for the next three months but I am assigned to stay at this Station. I'll be able to work on the EMS room and on my supply chain organization with no disruption.

I was watching one of my favorite movies, *Bridge of Spies,* again at St. Paul Fire the other day and it made me contemplate the value of my work. I hope I've used my life to contribute to society. My other two favorite movies are *Miracle on 34ᵗʰ Street* and *To Kill a Mockingbird.* All three movies are about lawyers trying to help the world. In *Miracle on 34ᵗʰ Street,* the lawyer has faith in people, particularly in Santa Claus and those who believe in goodness and kindness. In *To Kill a Mockingbird,* the attorney wanted justice for the oppressed and disenfranchised and a good life for his community and family. In *Bridge of Spies,* the lawyer brought people together to free human beings from prison and to help a college student. Each of these movies reminds me of how much I want to bring good to my community and the people I touch every day in my various roles as medic, lawyer, and theologian. I seem to fail a lot, but, like Scout, I have hope for both the present and the future. I believe we can all have hope for ourselves and for our world. In that hope, we should find compassion for all humankind. Compassion is showing concern, sensitivity, mercy, and kindness to others. It's when we recognize a need and take action to help.

Have faith and hope, show compassion, love, and charity. Instead of wealth, measure your success by your kindness to others. Take action today.

We just had a challenging call for a sick baby. The call was way outside of our district for a neighboring fire department. When we got there, we found a baby in a car who had been sick and is now lethargic after vomiting. We moved the baby to the medic and when I examined her, I found her to be having a seizure. We transported the child code 3 (red lights and sirens) and I advised the hospital we were coming in with a seizure. The child looked fine and would then close her eyes and have a focal seizure where her eyes deviated and flickered for about 10 seconds. I administered oxygen, got the infant BVM out, and gave her a puff or so when she would seize. Her oxygen saturation stayed at 99-100% the entire time. We did get out a CBG and prepped for an IO, but never had time to attempt it by the time we pulled in to the hospital. My focus was on the airway since the focal events only lasted for a few seconds at a time. Dr. Clothier was happy with the care we provided.

The Lord will look out for you and protect you, His love endures forever, and he will not abandon you.

Psalm 138:8

Whenever I have calls like this, I am thankful for the love of God and for all God's help in letting my knowledge, experience, and skills be used to the utmost. I also believe my angels, Dad, and Victor 3 are looking out for me as well. This is the greatest job—I get to take care of people and really make a difference in their lives. Most of the time, people don't even know what we've done and how strong we have been to take care of them or their loved one. It's a tough job, but somebody has got to do it! There is fulfillment in doing this work along with great joy. Thank you to all who have helped me get here.

June 30, 2017
Friday

After the last call where we got to help someone, we then had a call of great sadness. It was a CPR call and upon our arrival, we found the person had already died. We pronounced and then tried to help the spouse as much as we could. The death was a total surprise for the family. Everyone was in shock and dismay. I was deeply saddened.

We just had a complex call for someone who was on dialysis and missed a treatment. The woman had been to the dentist to have some teeth pulled earlier in the week and today came down with a 104° temperature. A diabetic on oxycodone, she was barely responsive. Her potassium was likely extremely high as well.

Sleep well and be thankful.

July

July 1, 2017
Saturday

WE STARTED OUT THIS MORNING AT 9:00 a.m. and have been running calls ever since. I think we are at 12 calls so far in 15 hours, including an out-of-town transport.

I worked with Stacy and Richard on the last call which was a trauma

Stacy and Richard, the best of the best!

entry. They are the greatest med techs and work so hard while being cheerful at the same time. I'm pleased to have finally gotten a picture of them together. Thank you both for being so awesome!

JULY 4, 2017
Tuesday – Happy 4ᵗʰ of July!

I AM SO THANKFUL FOR THE United States of America. I am free here and can work as hard as I can in order to succeed. We had the 4ᵗʰ of July Parade this morning in Mount Angel and, in my opinion, it's one of the best. The entire community lines the street to watch it. With the American Legion in the lead, a long line of jeeps, tanks, Army trucks, fire trucks, the rescue, old cars, tractors, and lots of floats follow them. From the fire truck and rescue, we all wave while tossing candy and the 1ˢᵗ Citizen and the Jr. 1ˢᵗ Citizen ride on top of the rescue which I get to drive. Between the wonderful parade and the beautiful day, sunny and warm, everything was pretty much perfect.

While there, I saw my teacher, Mr. Piatz, and my neighbor, Mr. Seiler, and I took a photo with them. Mr. Piatz taught me the importance of being strong and having character. For example, Mr. Piatz would never go to a tavern in Mt. Angel as the appearance of him there would be improper as a teacher. He held himself to the highest standards and taught me to remember that an appearance is

Charlotte and Sam rode in Rescue 454 with me, waving and tossing candy

as important as the facts for they can both harm a person. Of all the people I have ever known, Mr. Piatz holds himself to the very highest standards of character and integrity. (Mr. Piatz—I still remember you buying me a milkshake

Mr. Piatz and Mr. Seiler

when we went to a track meet in Molalla. Thank you.)

Mr. Seiler is my neighbor. He gave me my first haircut and then cut my hair for the next 45 years until he retired. I tell him I haven't had a good haircut since. I remember how after every haircut Dad would pay a dollar for the haircut and Mr. Seiler would slip a nickel in my hand for a candy. Thank you Mr. Seiler. He, too, has always been a solid person. His son Don and grandson Dean both volunteer with the Mt. Angel Fire Department and look out for me. Don and Dean have inherited the strong character and integrity of Mr. Seiler.

Mrs. Buchheit is another precious person in my life. She has prayed every day for me since 2015 that I would find the right job. After the parade, I stopped to see her and wish her a wonderful 4th of July. I told her to keep praying for me and she replied that she didn't know if they were working. I told her, "Yes, they are. We are just traveling on the Lord's train schedule and it's a bit slower than mine. Keep praying." You, too, can keep praying for me. I am in a perfect place at Marion County Fire; I hope to get to stay there for a long time. Good work Mrs. Buchheit. Thank you God for all you have done for me. God bless America and God bless you.

◆◆◆

I AM WORKING AT THE ST. Paul Rodeo this afternoon. I worked on Sunday and then tonight I work the chutes. St. Paul Fire provides all the medical staff for the event. Mark Daniel worked with me on the ambulance yesterday when we had three transports to the hospital. Tonight Mark and I will be working the rodeo chutes with the Justin Boots rodeo medical team.

I am so thankful to be working at Marion County Fire District #1. Yes, I am a probie, but I like to mop floors, empty the garbage, and take care of the dishes. Captain Deleon, who usually gives me the hardest time, told me he and the other guys wouldn't do it if they didn't like me. I saw my Fire Chief during my last tour when some "challenge coins" were handed out for the life we saved on July 1st and Salem Fire overlooked Bentz and me. I told him it was okay, that the best part of saving that man's life after he died in front of us was reviving him and bringing him back to life!

> *Blessed is the nation whose God is the Lord, the people he chose for his inheritance.*
>
> *Psalm 33:12*

JULY 5, 2017
Wednesday

MATT GOT HIS BLACK HELMET AND firefighter badge today! We're working together this shift and our first call of the day came in at 6:35 a.m. so Matt and I took it so the other medics could go home. On one of our trips to the hospital, I saw Devin for the first time in a long time. She is an awesome RN and has always been my friend and supporter. Thanks, Devin.

Devin, Registered Nurse, BSN

This is the perspective Mark Daniel and I had while working in the chutes.

Matt Bentz, James Lang, and me

Our most recent call was for a person who was tased by police after harassing his ex-girlfriend. Lang helped on that one. He is a solid medic who was promoted to firefighter in January. Matt, as you know, is solid as well and I am happy for the both of them.

I also got my supply order out this afternoon. Now I need to create a spreadsheet for the account manager. This helps us keep track of what was ordered and which invoice we should pay when the supplies come in. This is where I want to be and who I want to work with and who I want as my Chief Officers and leaders. I just hope I can still work at making a difference for the District and my patients along with working with them on highway safety.

As the announcer said at the close of the rodeo, "It is not about making money, it is about people."

July 6, 2017
Thursday

THE DAY HAS REMAINED STEADY WITH calls. Troy, who manages all the facilities, engines, and trucks, was on the engine for a few hours. He is typically very busy but found the time to run some calls with us, even making lunch and sharing it with the crew. A hard worker, it's always great to have him on a medical or fire scene.

We are back from our last call and it's a little after 10:00 p.m. I am ready to rest. The floors are mopped, the garbage is emptied, and the medic is restocked and fueled. Good night.

July 7, 2017
Friday

IT IS 12:13 A.M. AND I just finished my chart. We took in a severely intoxicated person to the hospital on whom I started an intravenous line and delivered a bolus of fluid. I don't understand why people like to get so intoxicated. He told me he was depressed about not being allowed to see his daughter. Okay, so he wants to see his daughter but getting so intoxicated that he can't even stand helps the situation? No, it does not help *any* situation. Throughout my career, I have heard this so many times. They won't let me do such and such so I am acting irresponsibly by getting very intoxicated and thus not helping the situation at all but making it worse. The more you want something, the more responsible you must become to achieve and gain what you desire. Pray for the misguided and the broken.

I am not anywhere close to being perfect. I am discouraged and sad and I occasionally feel hopeless. But so many people are good to me. They all give me strength and hope, and they all believe in me. I have noted many of them in these writings and extend my deepest gratitude to all of them. Above all is the love of God. Remember:

It reaches to the highest mountain,
and it flows to the lowest valley;
the blood that gives me strength
from day to day,
it will never lose its power.

Andraé Crouch

I ultimately find hope and strength in the Lord. I am so imperfect yet I am loved and cared for by God. We can all find peace in Him amidst our troubles and doubts. Another favorite song of mine is *Victory in Jesus.* The words bring strength and help me believe I will ultimately find victory.

Flower from Victor 3 tree

VICTORY IN JESUS

I heard an old, old story,
How a Savior came from glory,
How He gave His life on Calvary
To save a wretch like me;
I heard about His groaning,
Of His precious blood's atoning,
Then I repented of my sins
And won the victory.

Chorus:
O victory in Jesus,
My Savior, forever.
He sought me and bought me
With His redeeming blood;

He loved me ere I knew Him
And all my love is due Him,
He plunged me to victory,
Beneath the cleansing flood

I heard about His healing,
Of His cleansing pow'r revealing.
How He made the lame to walk again
And caused the blind to see;
And then I cried, "Dear Jesus,
Come and heal my broken spirit,"
And somehow Jesus came and bro't
To me the victory.

Chorus:
O victory in Jesus,
My Savior, forever.
He sought me and bought me
With His redeeming blood;
He loved me ere I knew Him
And all my love is due Him,
He plunged me to victory,
Beneath the cleansing flood.

E. M. Bartlett

Paul, my
awesome son

MCFD#1

As I told Matt Bentz today, we are so fortunate to be here at Marion County Fire. There is no other place I want to be in my life right now but here taking care of people and working on projects. Today Matt helped me with some of my projects. He's a smart guy and helped me with my computer work. In the afternoon, he gave a talk about water hydraulics, nozzles, and things to consider when fighting a fire. It was an excellent talk and showed superb preparation.

I truly have the best job.

Beauty found in life and nature

Love, give, forgive, help others, believe, have hope, and find strength in God.

5:28 A.M.

CODE SAVE! MATT AND I HAD another code save! A 65 year old woman had difficulty breathing all night and called us in the morning. By the time we arrived, the patient was in full cardiac arrest. I got the IO in the tibia and Matt ran the code. We got her pulse back and transported her to the hospital. When we left the hospital, the patient was awake. She will go home in a day or two and be just fine.

We are back and have already restocked the medic. I am glad we got the station cleaned up last night so all we have to do now is write charts and do a final cleanup.

On the way back to the station this morning, we treated ourselves by stopping for donuts. I bought a maple bar and Coke and Matt got a maple bar and a Dr. Pepper. Sometimes, I call a Coke and donut the breakfast of champions, or in this case, life savers.

In all, we ran 15 transports on this tour. With all those patients, it's been nice to trade back and forth with Matt.

Good morning and good night. I am going home to sleep.

July 11, 2017
Tuesday

Today I met with the Oregon Transportation Safety Committee at DPSST. Running the meeting can be tiresome. The information delivered was complicated and a lot to take in. We talked about legislation, administrative rules, strategic planning, and managing the safety action plan for best outcomes. The OTSC is responsible for highway safety in Oregon. When people die in accidents, it's very sad for their families and friends. Vision Zero has a goal of eliminating all deaths and serious injuries by an endpoint date of 2035 while my Outcome Zero® is one day at a time. I want to get all boys and girls, moms and dads, and friends and family home today and so we are searching to find measures and countermeasures to get people home safe. In many states, no day is death free. Here in Oregon, though, we are able to do this about 150 days a year. I want even more days of friends and families all making it home safe. Deputy Chief Kyle McMann has been great in helping me get time off to attend the meetings and I greatly appreciate his efforts.

In the afternoon I went to Station 1 to work on Medic 31. Moments after I had changed from my suit and tie to my uniform, we got a call and have been on calls ever since. Sometimes the calls are very difficult. I had a call earlier for a very sick woman with shortness of breath who waited and waited to call 911 until it was too late. We worked so hard to make her better but she stopped breathing as we reached the hospital;

she is in ICU now with a guarded outcome. I told Dr. Brian Clothier how difficult such a case is on me tonight. He looked at me and said it is difficult for him too. It is difficult for all the physicians when this happens to them. Dr. Clothier was my medical director and supervising physician at my previous ambulance company and has always supported me even when I occasionally disagreed with him at meetings.

JULY 12, 2017
Wednesday

WE HAVE BEEN ON CALLS SINCE 4:30 this morning after finishing up our last call at 12:30 last night and then we restocked the medic. I was in the administration office hallway moving boxes to the EMS room when Fire Chief Terry Riley saw me, stopped what he was doing, and came over to help. His practice of servant leadership constantly impresses me. He truly helps his people. He doesn't walk past work but stops to help. He helped at the pancake breakfast, hauled barrels around for the food drive, and was here for all the open houses. It makes me proud to be on his team. Thanks Chief.

IT'S NOW PAST 8:00 P.M. AND we are finally able to get back to work on our charts after we get a quick bite to eat. We also need to go over the drill information we missed while running our calls and covering for the other medics when they were drilling and running calls of their own. I suspect it will remain busy the rest of the night. Luckily, I have no plans for tomorrow so I'll be able to rest then. I also need to go over to the EMS room and get a pallet and a half of supplies checked in, audited, and stored.

I took care of a bicyclist who was hit by a car and was injured. He will be okay. I took care of the patient while Matt drove and I got everything done by the time we got to the hospital. Doctor Clothier was there to receive him and Stacey was there as the RN to manage the trauma team.

This tour has been non-stop since I got here yesterday. Notwithstanding, I want to work here and volunteer in Mt. Angel and nowhere else. Please pray for all the paramedics, firefighters, and EMTs tonight.

July 14, 2017
Friday
I AM AT THE EXPO CENTER for the Antique Show. I enjoy looking at all the items for sale and found many fun things but most cost more than I cared to spend. Many people have passed my office carrying their own finds out the door. Some are buying to take back to their stores and others are taking their goodies home to enjoy. I did find a clock I thought looked like fun and David Grant from Scappoose Fire gave me a reasonable price so I bought it. I figured it would be fun for my birthday.

I also enjoy finding fire nozzles every once in a while and am always looking for patches and badges. On occasion, I have found a fire extinguisher I can afford.

Two nozzles, a helmet, and a bag of rocks

I stayed at the station yesterday on my own time to get the EMS room straightened out. I was able to get all the supplies checked in and the paperwork turned into accounting. Then I stocked the shelves so the crews have enough supplies to get them through the next four days. After that, I went home to sleep the rest of the day. In the evening, I went down to Mt. Angel Fire and checked in the supplies there too. I will get the fire truck stocked when I'm there on Saturday.

JULY 16, 2017
Sunday – Happy Birthday to me!

I AM 64 YEARS OLD TODAY. Every year, I strive to have these qualities in my life:

- Resilience
- Steadfastness
- Dedication
- Tenacity
- Perseverance
- Compassion
- Respect
- Courtesy
- Consideration
- Patience
- Fun

I want these qualities to be a part of me and have had different people tell me I was all of these at one time or another.

Doctor Nicole Vanderheyden, MD, a trauma surgeon, and I are both resilient. We recently talked about how some people have resilience built into them. Sixty-four years ago today I was immediately baptized by the nurse when I was born. Premature and with birth defects, I was not expected to live through the day but I surprised them. When I was a little older, Mom was watching the neighborhood kids out on the river at their special swimming hole when I nearly drowned. I was in an old tire inner tube and slipped through the tube and couldn't swim. They pulled me out and took me to the hospital. From then on, I seemed susceptible to breathing problems and was diagnosed with asthma.

Of course, having had 63 surgeries from 5 to 15 years old taught me a lot about pain, suffering, and perseverance. More than once I became friends with other kids in the hospital who then died and were gone the next day or on my next visit to the hospital.

I remember waking up one time in a post-surgery haze with a boy jumping up and down in my bed, his head wrapped like mine. My mother and his mother were sitting and talking. The next morning I went to find him and was told he had died overnight from brain cancer. Another boy I would push around in his wheelchair until his mother arrived in the afternoon. He would eat with a fork and knife but then his mom would let him eat fried chicken with his fingers. I don't know if that is where I got the habit of using a fork and knife with everything, including pizza, but I do! We saw each other every 2-3 months in the hospital. Then one day when I was watching for my dad who was picking me up in his semi-truck to take me home. I was so excited to see him pull up, I grabbed a nurse to get me down to the lobby. Unfortunately, I was so rushed that I didn't say goodbye to my friend. When I returned a few months later, I found out he had died.

When I responded to the motor vehicle crash in 1991, I thought that was the most excruciating thing to ever happen to me. My dad was dead and Paul was all but dead. I survived. Then on January 2, 2009, Victor 3 was in a crash and when I arrived at the hospital to be at his side, I found he had already died. Doctor Vanderheyden was actually the one to break the news to me. I kissed Victor 3's forehead for the last time in Room 7 of Salem Hospital. The sadness I felt was and still is indescribable.

I went back to taking care of people. Some days I don't understand how I do it, how I keep myself together and do what I do best—taking care of people. I think that I must be resilient. Somehow, I have held onto my compassion all these years, though I am challenged some days to show it.

Everyone has struggles. Somehow, most of us get through them. All I know is to have faith and hope, to give and forgive, to help others and to have charity for all and to give all people respect and courtesy.

July 17, 2017
Monday

MATT BOUGHT ICE CREAM AND THE station crew sang *Happy Birthday* to me tonight. Yes, 64 years old and going all day long with lots of calls including one stroke patient.

Matt is thoughtful to take care of me in that way. He is kind and we work well together.

A friend was in earlier to say hello and he mentioned the term, "legacy." I have been thinking about what *my* legacy might be one day. For me, I think it would be my children. Both Victor 3 and Paul were great boys when growing up in Mount Angel. Victor 3 was wonderful and worked so hard as an Army officer. He made me proud. Paul continues to look out for people and show kindness. He particularly takes care of and looks out for me. Earlier today, Paul called to wish me a happy birthday. I hope to go down and watch a Utah football game with him this fall. I am so proud of him.

I have asked myself numerous times if what I have done in 64 years means anything. I hope I've made a difference but sometimes I'm not sure. Most of the time, I do believe I've been able to touch people's lives. Sometimes I have saved a life, other times I have

64 years old and working strong at MCFD#1

delivered a baby, or held a hand to give support and comfort. I hope that, ultimately, I am regarded as a dedicated community servant.

♦♦♦

We have just returned from Salem Hospital Emergency after taking several serious patients there throughout this afternoon and evening. One of them is probably going to die. He has brain cancer and no one knew this until tonight after a CT scan was done. It's a sad situation for both him and his family. He may never recover or make it home. We have taken in other people who are not as sick who will be fine after a little doctoring and some tender loving care from the nursing staff. I am praying for that man and his family.

While we were at the hospital, I saw two of my favorite nurses, Kelly and Steve, who have been great supporters of mine when I was struggling to find a place to work that would hire me. Too often, I was either too old, too educated, or too experienced. Kelly and Steve have great faith in me and their support has never wavered no matter how I was feeling. When MCFD#1 hired me, they were among the first to celebrate and encourage me to be strong. They are solid people and have helped me to be a solid person. They have always offered me encouragement whenever I see them and they always tell me I do a great job taking care of our patients. My deepest gratitude to you both.

JULY 18, 2017
Tuesday

GOOD MORNING. WE HAVE ALREADY RUN several calls this morning and transported patients to the hospital. Two of our calls were actually for the same person six hours apart. She was released from the hospital and then wandered away from her house before someone called 911 for her. Her family is not interested in being her caregivers and seem to just push her out of the house to wander or call 911 themselves. I asked the social worker to intervene and help find a solution for the patient.

I am reminded this morning of how thankful I am to be here at Marion County Fire. My pay may be inequitable right now but I have hope the promises to correct that for me will be kept. I do not want to be anywhere else.

Just before this last call came in, I was about to mop the floor. I'm now going to go finish that up. Everyone be strong, thankful, and believe in the future.

WE HAVE BEEN ON A LIFT assist and shortly we will take the engine out to the Boy Scouts to give them a tour. The Boy Scouts are having a jamboree behind the station where there is a large area for them to do all their activities.

Kelly, me, and Steve

I had a great talk earlier tonight with a firefighter about equity and he helped me realize what is most important to me here at MCFD#1. Pay equity is not as important to me as simply being here. Cleaning, mopping, and taking care of things here at the station are important. I have heard stories of lazy probies and really don't want to be one of those stories in the future.

I was given a new assignment by the Battalion Chief this morning. Being a valuable and productive member of the District is important to me. Running calls, taking care of people, problem solving, and using critical thinking skills is why I'm here. I love working for MCFD#1.

JULY 23, 2017
Sunday

WE ARE HAVING A TERRIFIC MORNING. We first checked the ambulance out and restocked it with supplies. We then had a drill where we practiced taking a hydrant and pulling a cross-lay. Matt did all the pulling and I rolled up the hose and helped with the cross-lay restoration. We then washed dishes and cleaned the kitchen. This afternoon we are having a lunch meeting with the Battalion Chief and Matt and I were put in charge of the side dishes and dessert so we went to the store to buy what we needed: multiple kinds of potato salad along with coleslaw and ice cream bars for dessert. The engine crew is in charge of sandwiches.

We have accomplished a lot of things this morning. We got through drill while it was still cool, washed both the medic and engine, and both Matt and Mikey, who is a student Captain from Chemeketa Community College, helped me with the EMS room and now all I have to do is Monday's paperwork. (As a side note, Mikey is now a career firefighter with MCFD#1 and remains the hardest working probie ever.)

Hear me Lord, and be kind and gracious to me; My Lord, be my helper and supporter, protect me. You have turned my pain and sorrow into a smile and gladness; you have removed my sackcloth and clothed me with happiness and joy; that my heart and soul may sing and not be silent. Lord my God, I will thank you and praise you forever.

Psalms 30:10-12

♦♦♦

Just as we started the meeting, we got a call to transport a patient to the hospital. They saved us some food and the meeting was brief. It is past 5 p.m. now and I think I will work out and then rest.

♦♦♦

We have run some calls and finished cleaning the administration building. Chemeketa Fire Captain Mikey Finneran helped clean up the building and then finished it by himself while we ran to the hospital.

We had a code 3 call for someone with both a breathing problem and a seizure. Everything went well and the patient was fine by the time we got to the hospital.

Connie Jo, our wonderful cookie lady, brought cookies for us to eat. She brings them in as a thank you for all we do for the community. Thanks Connie Jo! They were delicious!

I haven't worked out yet because we were cleaning the admin building when we got a code 3 call. I think I'll get a snack and watch *Columbo* with Peter Falk. Peter is an inspiration. He wanted to be on television and in the movies but was told to forget it as he only had one eye. Peter persevered, though, and became very successful. Throughout his career he played lots of characters besides Columbo including an angel in a Christmas movie on The Hallmark Channel, *When Angels Come to Town*. The movie is one of my favorites. "Just keep trying," is the key to life, success, and personal fulfillment, plus faith, hope, and charity.

July 24, 2017
Monday

It has been a fantastically busy day. First thing this morning, we had an early drill at 8:00 a.m. at College Station. Then by 8:32 we got a demanding CPR call for a 25 year old who was unconscious and barely breathing. After cleaning up the mess in the ambulance and then restocking it at Station 1, we returned to drill. This time, we drilled another 30 minutes or so then all three medics were called out along with both engines. This call was for a nice man with dementia who tripped and fell at his adult foster care home. It appeared he dislocated his shoulder so we got the arm sling and I started an intravenous line for a dose of Fentanyl to help with his pain. He felt much better after the Fentanyl.

Ashley went over the durable supply budget and the particulars of the program as her last day of work is coming up soon. She has taken a job at the airport for the Port of Portland so I will be taking over the durable supply project from now on. As you know, the disposable supply job is a full-time job. It involves keeping the EMS room stocked for the other crews, ordering supplies so we don't run out, anticipating what we'll need to order so we have enough even with all the backorder problems we have with suppliers, checking the supplies in once they arrive, and completing the accounting paperwork so the suppliers are paid in a timely manner.

◆◆◆

I'm tired. We just got back from three calls and I am now finished with all my charts and had a snack. I am going to rest now for a while. So far, we were called out to a motorcycle crash, a fall, and an alarm sounding. Tonight I have an air show meeting to get ready for the air show in September. Thank God for a great tour. Please go out and bless people with kindness, charity, and understanding.

July 29, 2017
Saturday

> *The Lord has told us what we should do: See that justice is done, do what is right for other people, let mercy be your first concern, show compassion and loving kindness, be humble and walk with God.*
>
> *Micah 6:8*

I saw my Fire Chief in Mount Angel on Wednesday when he came over for the Marion County Fire Chief's Defense Board meeting. Then we drilled outside on medical emergencies. After the meeting, I had a nice talk with both of the Chiefs and it reminded me how fortunate I am to be with Marion County Fire District #1 and Mt. Angel Fire District #15 where I get to help my hometown community and Marion County. A recent article I read talked about educating oneself and becoming the boss. That is what most people want to do in EMS but I want to stay in the battle and be a street medic. I have the education to move up the ladder but I find moving up often

Fire Chief Trierweiler, me, and Fire Chief Riley

changes a person and their attitudes. Whether you are a field medic or a manager, you can be a leader from the field by maintaining compassion for the patients and their families. Somehow, people become bitter, angry, and biased against other people. They forget why they wanted to be a firefighter or paramedic in the first place. Though they start out wanting to help, they now feel entitled and nasty. Sometimes I do wonder if I should have jumped into an office 20 years ago and learned how to be an awful person but I think I would have held on tight to respect and courtesy no matter where I was working. Many people do hold strong and stay compassionate. In my experience, though, many also become evil.

I've been thinking about the journey I've taken these last few months as a probie. It feels a bit discombobulated and confusing to me but perhaps that is what a journey is: walking and crawling and running and moving, usually forward rather than backwards. A journey is the act of traveling from one place to another and I have certainly done that. Like a hiking trail, the path moves around and isn't always clear. At times I have been discouraged, then happy, then sad, and then happy again, but no matter what the surroundings are, the path goes on.

I now have two months left on probation and then many months and years to continue to do my very best. That's my commitment to excellence. That's my journey today. Though the journey started 64 years ago, it continues today to a place I do not know. I have overcome many obstacles. I've been told I was ugly and stupid. I've been belittled by teachers and told by counselors I wouldn't ever accomplish anything because I was a cripple. But I am determined to prove them wrong every day I am gifted with being upon this earth. There is still so much I want to do with my life, love and service I want to give my community. To do it all, I plan to live another 40 years. I believe that raising two good boys is a wonderful accomplishment and that saving lives and delivering babies in the most difficult of situations is an accomplishment as well. I believe that holding an elderly person's hand and giving reassurance is something good and I hope that by doing these things, my life has meant something.

My journey continues and I don't mind that I don't always know where I am going for that is what life is: an adventurous journey. Have hope and faith and love. I hope to have hope and faith and love forever.

As water reflects the face, so one's life reflects the heart.
Proverbs 27:19

Bless my heart Lord, please, bless my heart.

Demonstrate love and be inclusive to all people. Regardless of whether or not you agree with someone else, love them. Let the love of God show through you and all you do today and every day.

July 30, 2017
Sunday

THIS TOUR HAS TURNED INTO A busy 24 hours. Starting last night at 6:00 p.m. until a day later at 9:00 p.m. on Sunday night, we have had call after call after call and each one seems a little more tragic than the last.

Our first call was for a young man who was smoking marijuana. Unfortunately, it must have had an herbicide or pesticide all over the stuff for he had an allergic reaction and his whole face was terribly swollen. Next, we had a call for a woman who had overdosed on heroin but when we arrived at the scene, the person was just shaky. We talked to her and found out that she was experiencing pain but her doctor would not give her any more pain medicine. He just cut her off! It's a problem I've seen before. Without pain medication, she turned to heroin, I believe. People get hooked on medications and the drug companies make money. Now doctors are forced to withhold the medication rather than help these people.

Furthermore, it's no longer the doctors who run medicine but the insurance companies.

A similar situation of carelessness is that a friend of mine needs surgery for her knees but the insurance company won't authorize it as just giving her drugs to deal with the pain is cheaper. This is plain stupid and should be illegal. Medical necessity means nothing to insurance companies; it's cheaper to get people hooked on drugs rather than to actually treat them correctly. This particular patient was emaciated, sick, and shaking. She had taken half a dose of heroin for her pain and the self-righteous medical system won't help her overcome her addiction which they caused in the first place. So often it seems that insurance executives prefer greed over doing the right thing. My friend suffers every day due to their greed. Insurance companies ought to be ashamed.

Our next call was for an older woman who had been sick with a fever and possible infection who finally called for help. We got her taken care of and had returned to the station to catch up on our charting when we got another call for a breathing problem. On the way to that call, it was changed from the breathing problem to a CPR call. The family was hysterical when we arrived. The volunteer engine crew immediately began compressions and I started the intraosseous line to administer medications to the 52 year old man. We all worked feverishly but in the end, we had to stop the resuscitation and pronounce him deceased. That is not easy for me and not easy for the team. My heart was sad for the family and their loss.

After getting back to the station and restocking the medic, we got another call that was, thankfully, simple and everything turned out well.

After all those calls, we were finally able to go back to the station for some rest at 4:30 a.m. The next morning we were to have our team Sunday breakfast meeting when another CPR call came in. This time we arrived to find a woman who had just discovered a deceased friend who had likely died the day before. The woman told us how her friend had been unemployed for the last six months and just found a new job which she was supposed to be starting the next day. Apparently, she had just returned from trying out the commute from Salem to Portland to test how long it would take to get there before she arrived home, collapsed, and died. Oh my gosh, I felt so sad.

We have such a great team. They all look out for each other and particularly for me, the now 64 year old probie. Battalion Chief Bjorklund, my EMS Chief, is always good to me and they were all very comforting to our team.

Our next two calls were for diabetics. One was for low blood sugar and the other was for high blood sugar. We transported the high blood sugar patient to the hospital and treated the low blood sugar patient as we could make him better right at home. Just as we got back from those calls, we got another for a motor vehicle crash out on Highway 22. Aumsville Fire arrived to the scene right before we did and found there weren't any injuries so we were able to cancel the call and clear it with the Oregon State Police.

The calls would simply not stop. Our next one was for a person on the soccer field who needed treatment and transport to the hospital for heat stroke. As we pulled back in to the station to park, we got yet another call for a sick person. As it turned out, this person was extremely sick and may have meningitis.

Our last call was for a 52 year old man who had a heart attack. I called a STEMI Alert (ST Elevation Myocardial Infarction) which means that the cath lab is notified to prepare for the patient. We had to use the pacer on him on the way to the hospital as his heartbeat dropped down to the 40s and he had no pulse as he talked to us in the ambulance. We later found out he'd had a 99% occlusion of his coronary artery and died in the cath lab three hours later. This tour is taking a toll on both my brain and especially on my heart. Too many people have died this weekend.

Now it's Sunday night and I am going to watch the last half of *Columbo* before taking a nap. As the song, "Take My Hand, Precious

Lord," goes, "I am tired, I am weak, I am worn." I am thankful the Lord holds me up and gives me strength.

> *It is God who gives you strength and helps you stand firm in Christ. He anointed you, set his seal of love and ownership on you, he put his Spirit in your heart as a promise as to what is to come for you.*
>
> *2 Corinthians 1:21-22*

GOOD MORNING, IT'S 3:30 A.M. NOW. We just took in an 81 year old woman who had been suffering with terrible, unrelenting abdominal pain all day and couldn't take it any longer. It turns out she was having a severe gallbladder attack. Doubled over in pain and vomiting, we got her into the ambulance and Matt started an intravenous line for me while I pulled out some drugs to make her feel better. He hopped into the driver's seat and starting transporting us to the hospital while I administered Fentanyl for her pain and Zofran for her nausea and vomiting. When we arrived at the hospital, she thanked us for our care. Her pain was diminished, she had stopped vomiting, and was no longer nauseous. Success! Woo hoo! Now for a nap.

August

AUGUST 1, 2017
Tuesday

TODAY WE HAD FOUR CALLS IN Mt. Angel and I went out on all four of them. In the evening, we took the fire engine to National Night Out where the police and fire district hosted a barbecue and displays. I pumped water with the engine so all the children could try knocking over a traffic cone with the water spray from the fire hose and nozzle. Watching the kids smile as they try to knock over the cones is always so much fun! One little boy giggled and hugged his mom after knocking over the cone. It was awesome. After an hour and a half and 430 gallons of water sprayed, everyone had enjoyed multiple chances to knock over the cone. We then refilled the engine and went back to the station. I feel such joy helping the kids spray water and seeing their excitement!

August 2. 2017
Wednesday

This morning I went to the union meeting before taking my new suit by the tailor's shop to have the pants hemmed and the coat tailored. I've needed a new suit for some time and found this one for $75. I then went over to Station 1 to check on my supply orders and to restock the EMS room for the crews. While I was there, I stopped by the station house to send in a supply order instead of waiting for my shift on Friday. Captain Deleon found me there and asked me to work Medic 32 tonight and so now I'm here at Station 2. Though I missed the Mt. Angel Fire meeting tonight, Battalion Chief Milano understands my desire to work hard and how much I like being here at MCFD#1. He is very smart and well educated and understands my desire to take care of people. It was good to have a casual talk with him about our work.

> *Don't act out of selfish ambition or vain conceit. Rather, be humble and value others above yourself, don't worry about your own interest but look out for others, put their interests first.*
>
> Philippians 2:3

I am going to cover the shifts of a couple new firefighter candidates tomorrow so they can complete their testing. Say a prayer for me please.

August 5, 2017
Saturday

The closing of my mother's estate is almost over. I am looking forward to being done for people's meanness is overwhelming, though not surprising. Unfortunately, things have gone exactly as I told my mother they would. While I know I shouldn't allow people to treat me in this way, it seems some people *want* to cause chaos and find delight in hurting others. I should be strong and not frustrated, I know. I'll continue to do my best and believe. I need to remember Isaiah 62:5, "As a bridegroom rejoices over his bride, so will God rejoice over you." God *does* love us and will help us overcome, to be strong, and have faith. In the meantime, go out and help someone in some small way. Small acts can make gigantic differences in the life of another.

WE DIDN'T GET MUCH REST LAST night as we went out on a lot of calls. In between, I was able to check off two pallets of supplies and to clean out all the empty boxes and debris around the EMS room. I also threw out a lot of outdated and broken supplies which have been sitting around for over a year. The room looks great now! We then had a fire call at 5:00 a.m. and then medical calls at 7:00 and 8:00.

I had just returned from a transport to Salem Hospital when I saw Captain Elmer from Salem Fire who came over to greet me and ask how I was doing. They had just returned from a major apartment fire where they were the first engine on the scene.

♦♦♦

IT'S NOW 3:11 A.M. AND IT'S been a busy evening. The medic is now restocked, the dishes are done, the floor is mopped, and I am going to rest as I work in St. Paul later today. Please be kind to everyone.

AUGUST 11, 2017
Friday
YESTERDAY WAS A GREAT DAY! WE were able to accomplish so many projects in the EMS room! I still have to repair several EKG monitors but that requires additional research first. Right now, I am negotiating

prices to help save budget money while still meeting the needs of the team.

One of our recent calls was for a woman who experienced nausea, vomiting, high blood sugar, and dehydration all at the same time along with bites from bed bugs. The house was infested with the little critters. Though the exterminators were scheduled to come and take care of the problem, they hadn't been there yet. She was really sick. We gave her Zofran and a bolus of normal saline intravenously to help her feel better while we took her to the hospital.

I was so happy by the time we left the hospital. While there, I saw several friends. Stacey was the PFC, Stacy and Richard were the Med-Techs running around and working hard as usual, Nathan was taking care of patients, and Katie, a paramedic and colleague, had just delivered a patient to the emergency department. Each person stopped to greet me and ask how I was doing. Several of them hugged me and all of them were so kind. After another difficult week, these friends lifted my spirits. Thank you all for your thoughtfulness.

I watched *Bridge of Spies* again on Sunday and it always makes me want to do more. Sometimes I feel like I haven't done anything but then I remind myself how I have been instrumental in saving lives, delivering babies, and helping people in their time of need. I have held patients' hands to provide comfort and distract them from their injuries and circumstances. Many patients have told me about their garden, their children, or how they love to go fishing. Sometimes patients have offered insights about their faith. Almost anyone can start an intravenous line or deliver a baby, but not just anyone can provide comfort and understanding in such circumstances. This, I believe, is my gift to patients.

Still, I want to do more for my community; I'm just not sure how. There is a job I would like to have—a brand new position with the Department of Justice in Salem called the Public Records Counsel. This person would be the mediator and decider in public records request disputes. I believe I would be great in that position as I have no political ambitions or desire to move up to a bigger job. I would have the courage and fortitude to make a decision that public agencies would not like me to make against them, particularly if they are trying to hide their misdeeds. I would be a guardian for the people. Still, I love the job I'm in. I've been taking care of people my whole life. Even as a child of eight back at Good Samaritan Hospital, I would eat my dinner and would then help the nurses by feeding the three year olds. A few years later, I volunteered at the Benedictine Nursing Home then worked as a hospital chaplain as an adult and have now worked as a medic and firefighter in Mt. Angel for the last 37 years. That is what I am good at—no, *great* at doing. Taking care of people is what I do best. Now I just need to figure out how to serve my community as I get older over the next 50 years.

While I've been contemplating all of this over the last few weeks, I've realized I have become far more of a philosophical person. Yes, I still mop floors, take the garbage out, and wash all the dishes, all of which I have done this morning, and I run medic calls and transport patients to the hospital, but I've been focusing more and more on equality, equity, and social justice. Am I going in the wrong direction by thinking about these things? This is what I want to hold onto in myself though—these deep thoughts and practical actions as I continue my journey and come through my struggles. Thus, I will continue to work hard to show respect and courtesy to all people while being inclusive and showing compassion for all while caring for each person who comes my way.

A number of years ago, I had the privilege to be the personal paramedic to the Dali Lama when he was here visiting Portland. I am a fan of his and love some of his sayings so it was a pleasure to attend his talk and be assigned to him in case he needed anything. The Dali Lama tells us our primary purpose in life is to help others and to be happy. No matter what your belief system is, having compassion for the poor, widows, children, the destitute, and the disenfranchised is important. So when the Dali Lama said, "If you want others to be happy, practice compassion. If you want to be happy, practice compassion." His words rang true to me.

In 1975, I heard the Reverend Doctor George O. Wood preach at Southern California College (now Vanguard University) at chapel about doing your best in spite of any obstacles placed in our paths. Over time, I know I've allowed some obstacles to jump into my path and have even caused some of them myself. So often, we are the cause of our own difficulties. During his talk he said that "What happens *in you* is more important than what happens *to you.*" My passion to care for people and my compassion for their plight has not wavered and it's stronger today than it's ever been. People have been mean to me since I was a child but I continue to believe in my own inherent worth as I work diligently to be a servant to my community. Though these last two years have been a huge challenge to everything I believe and feel about humankind, I am sure that whether it's at work or in the community, being a servant is what really matters. Being at Mt. Angel Fire and at Marion County Fire is where I want to be to serve my community. (When Oprah is President I am willing to be her personal paramedic, personal chaplain, personal lawyer, and a policy advisor.)

In Luke 22:26, Jesus says, "Let the person who is the greatest become the student, and the leader become the servant." This is what I have been trying to do. In my career, I used to be in higher positions. In fact, my Field Training Officer at Marion County Fire was initially trained by me years earlier. In addition, my colleagues at the academy were either trained or supervised by me at some point in our careers. Like Jesus said, the master became the student and the student became the master. From once holding the position of supervisor, I am now a probationary paramedic who cleans the floors, washes the dishes, and takes out the garbage. In that time, I have learned that a true leader should be a leader-servant like my Fire Chief who washes his own rig, hauls food barrels around, and serves pancakes. The last time the crews ate a meal with the Chief Officers, the Chief Officers insisted we eat first. When I stood back because I am the probie, they told me I must go before them and when I hesitated, they said they would not eat until all of the crew got food first. That is the leader-servant style of real leadership.

> *Whoever wishes to become a leader should be a servant; and whoever wishes to be the frontrunner should first be a servant to everyone. Because even Jesus did not come to earth to be served, but to serve, and to give His life for all.*
>
> *Mark 10:43-45*

In Mark 9:35-37, it says, "Jesus said to his disciples, 'If anyone wants to be first, let him be last of all and be the servant of all,' and taking a child into his arms Jesus said, 'Whoever receives one child like this in My name is receiving Me.'" We should all look for the needs of people in our communities, particularly the subtle needs of those people who need help and won't declare their difficulties. Please help those who are quietly suffering and trusting in God to bring them the help they need. My plan is to just keep doing the best I can in life, to be happy, strong, and not angry or bitter. Lord, help me to be strong.

As Angela Primm sings in *He Looked Beyond My Faults* and *Amazing Grace*, thank you, Lord, for looking beyond my faults and giving me your amazing grace.

AUGUST 17, 2017
Thursday

THERE IS AN ECLIPSE COMING in a few days on August 21, 2017 and Lynell's family are here visiting with us so they can see it. To entertain them in the meanwhile, we took them up to the Mt. Angel Abbey to visit the museum and to enjoy the view of the Willamette Valley from the hilltop. It's always a beautiful and peaceful place to go.

From the Abbey: an Angel, a flower, and a Victor talking machine from the museum

Today is Thursday and we have been moderately busy with calls, stocking the EMS room, checking in supplies, researching equipment to buy which will save us thousands of dollars, and having drills over the last two days. We've also added new straps to all of the stretchers which will be easier to clean and we made sure each medic has moving devices to help move patients easily and safely. Being in charge of durable medical equipment, I always try to find both the best quality and the best prices so everyone's job is easier.

Our first call yesterday morning was for a woman who fell and broke her hip. She was stepping out of her house and missed the step when it happened. I gave her pain and nausea medication to make her comfortable on the way in to the hospital. At Salem Emergency, all the great people were working. Though I've had occasional differences with the staff there, I believe I've been able to create a positive rapport with the great majority of them. Things always work out in the end for God has a plan for us all, even if it's at His speed and not ours. The staff there, both yesterday and today, are my favorite people and we appreciate each other's work. Knowing it gets terribly busy at the hospital, I always try to make the staff's job easier whenever I can. For example, today when I took someone in, I made sure I wrote my turnover report in the same order the computer program asks for it so the emergency staff knew just where to look if they had a question. I later took in a patient suffering from ventricular tachycardia (a fast-beating heart) and took a bunch of EKG tracings and 12-lead tracings. To make it easier for the nurses, I made sure to tape the tracings to the hospital's EKG strip paperwork and placed patient labels on them. (On the way to the hospital, we were able to slow his rhythm after which he felt much better and had no chest pain.) The staff there can see these efforts and appreciate how it helps them treat patients faster once we get them there.

In between all these calls, I saw Nancy Bee. She has always been a champion of mine and appreciates these efforts. One time I placed a pediatric C-Collar on an adult patient since the adult size was way too big and the child's size fit well. A nurse who no longer works there complained to Nancy about it and Nancy asked in reply, "Who was the medic?" and the nurse replied, "Victor." She then told the nurse, "Oh, Victor, then that is okay." Knowing me, she knew I had a reason for what I did and she believed in me. Nancy Bee is now the Nurse Manager, which is the top job, and is an awesome person and smart manager. Thank you, Nancy Bee. You bless me.

Matt and I have now finished stocking the backup medics with patient moving devices and new stretcher straps as well as revisiting the EMS room to tidy up and stock up on the supplies. A friend of mine who is redoing his EMT certification is riding with us today.

Though he has been retired, he was recently asked to take over as Fire Chief in a small department and he wants his EMT certification back as well so he can be of greater service to the community. It's been a joy to have him around.

We just came back from a CPR call but found the person had been dead for several hours before we were called in to help. We got there and confirmed he was dead before calling the Sheriff's Department to take over and investigate. Sometimes my work is sad.

August 18, 2017
Friday

WE HAVE JUST RETURNED FROM OUR last call of the tour. When I get off here, I'm heading up to the Convention Center for an eight hour shift. The job I do here at Marion County Fire, Mt. Angel Fire, and St. Paul Fire is so important to me. Most people do not understand me and my heart but here I get to help my community and that is what I want to do with my life. Regardless of the pay, I get the privilege of helping others in their time of distress. You have probably heard that people work to live, I work to give. My role in life is to give service to the needy and to be the servant of humankind. Like Don Quixote, I believe in good deeds and chivalry. The song "The Impossible Dream" from the *Man of La Mancha* beautifully describes my quest to be a servant of humankind.

> *To dream the impossible dream*
> *To fight the unbeatable foe*
> *To bear with unbearable sorrow*
> *To run where the brave dare not go*
> *To right the unrightable wrong*
> *To love pure and chaste from afar*
> *To try when your arms are too weary*
> *To reach the unreachable star*

This is my quest, to follow that star
No matter how hopeless, no matter how far
To fight for the right, without question or pause
To be willing to march into Hell, for a Heavenly cause
And I know if I'll only be true, to this glorious quest,
That my heart will lie peaceful and calm,
When I'm laid to my rest
And the world will be better for this:
That one man, scorned and covered with scars,
Still strove, with his last ounce of courage,
To reach the unreachable star.

I hope you understand me a little because I feel silly telling you about my desire to take care of people. My one regret is that the pay has prevented me from helping Lynell fulfill her dreams and hopes for her own life. Before her heart surgery, she ran a great athletic program at Willamette Valley Christian School, taught second grade, and still helps the church in numerous ways including being an integral part of Sunday worship. She is successful and loved by everyone but she, like me, wants to give so much more in her life. Yet I have failed her. We *both* have dreams of service.

AUGUST 18, 2017
Friday

I AM AT THE CONVENTION CENTER today where an international scientific seminar is wrapping up. Medically speaking, it's been pretty quiet so I have been listening to *Amazing Grace*.

Amazing Grace, how sweet the sound,
that saved a wretch like me.
I once was lost but now am found,
was blind, but now, I see.

*T'was Grace that taught
my heart to fear.
And Grace, my fears relieved.
How precious did that Grace appear
the hour I first believed.
Through many dangers, toils and snares
we have already come.
T'was Grace that brought us safe thus far
and Grace will lead us home.
The Lord has promised good to me
His word my hope secures.
He will my shield and portion be
as long as life endures.
When we've been there ten thousand years
bright shining as the sun.
We've no less days to sing God's praise
than when we've first begun.
Amazing Grace, how sweet the sound,
that saved a wretch like me.
I once was lost but now am found,
was blind, but now, I see.*

John Newton

My faith grows stronger listening to this hymn and many other songs as well. Lord, protect me, guide me, give me strength, give me knowledge and wisdom, and please let my experience and skills be present in my time of need.

There was an advertisement on YouTube for a movie. I missed the title but I saw a clip where the pastor said to his son, "Let's ask for God's help," and his son replied, "Aren't you God's help?" That's how I see myself; I try to help others when they need help. When someone has an emergency, they often pray for God's help and we show up to give it. Though we know we aren't God and people sometimes do die in spite of all the help we give, we do save lives and certainly provide comfort and peace of mind to many patients and their families. Please pray for all the firefighters, paramedics, and EMTs today and every day. I know that without the grace of God, I could not do what I do as a paramedic. Earlier today, someone observed to me that all the pain and suffering we see must affect us. Yes, it does affect us and after 37 years, I believe I wouldn't have made it this far without faith and God's love. Pray for all of the first responders serving your community and the world.

> *And God said to the people; Truly I say to you, whomever takes care of my children, whomever takes care of my brothers and sisters, the needy and the poor, even the least of them, you did it to Me.*
>
> *Matthew 25:40*

I will keep doing the best I can at my many jobs helping and serving God's children.

AUGUST 21, 2017
Monday – Total Eclipse

Photos of the total eclipse by NASA

August 22, 2017
Tuesday

Today has been one of the most frustrating days I've had at MCFD#1. For weeks now Matt and I have been trying to find ways to keep our durable supplies from breaking. In the end, we came up with two solutions. While they both would have saved money and maintained the integrity of the system, I thought one solution was better than the other but when I tried to tell the Battalion Chief why, he didn't listen and made a decision based solely on which one would save us more money. Of course, the solution he picked will work but it's not the one I wanted and I don't feel heard.

Another frustrating incident occurred when both engine Captains were there in the office and one asked me a question about a matter I had inquired about last week. He then turned to the Battalion Chief to follow the chain of command and told him I had a question. The Battalion Chief just looked at me and told me not to worry about it, that he already knew about the people I had a question about, all about me, and that he had contacts and connections no one knows about. This is the third time he's been abrupt with me in recent days. It's certainly a different type of leadership and management style than I am used to working with in the business world and I don't understand why he would behave that way towards me. I know I am just a probie and on the lowest rung of the ladder here but I *have* been doing this for a very long time and I don't like being talked down to as if I don't know anything.

A bright spot in the day happened later when I was working with Anita, the accounting specialist, on finding solutions to other budget issues. She helped me find what I wanted and helped me solve the problem. She is always helpful and I am grateful for her assistance.

♦♦♦

WE ARE BACK FROM A CALL now and I'm going to get some rest. My in-laws, who have been staying with us during their visit, came over to say goodbye before heading home. I have loved spending the last week with them at our home in Mt. Angel.

AUGUST 23, 2017
Wednesday

Nelda and John at Station 1

> *The name of the Lord is a strong tower of strength, the faithful shall run to it and will be safe.*
>
> *Proverbs 18:10*

GOOD MORNING. IT'S A BEAUTIFUL DAY and I want to thank you Lord for giving me strength.

We've had a busy day with our first call coming in at 4:03 a.m., another at 8:12 a.m., and then continuing on until just now when we finished our charts. We plan to eat breakfast for lunch and then I need to take care of the EMS room by checking in supplies and perhaps placing an order. I was able to get two orders placed yesterday but I have one more to take care of in order to meet the future needs of the agency.

One of our calls was for an unresponsive patient with severe bradycardia and no palpable pulse. Many times in past years I have jostled a person in bradycardia and they have responded with an increase in their pulse rate and blood pressure. I call this the "Victor Jiggle Method" and when we moved this man to the stretcher to carry him out of his room, we gave it a try and once again, it worked.

Troy is covering the firefighter position today and is in charge of eight stations, all the fire engines, medics, brush rigs and tenders, basically everything that is big and can break. He is extremely busy and is always working on multiple projects. Today he was with us and I always feel so safe and secure when he's around. Troy always has my back. I also took the opportunity to have a good talk with Captain Doeden who is now the new Captain at my station after switching stations with Captain Kettering earlier this month.

Matt and I spent about three hours in the EMS room checking in supplies and getting it stocked and organized. Matt, in particular, is great at organization and feng shui (风水拼写). The EMS room is now in harmony and balance. Between that, running calls, and going to a drill, it's been a fairly busy day.

AUGUST 24, 2017
Thursday

THIS LAST TOUR ALONG WITH THE last couple of tours have taken a toll on me. I have felt frustrated and hope to turn it around.

I've read numerous articles in the past about getting more education in order to become a manager instead of just a street medic. At times, it feels like the writers believe that staying a street medic is to have failed but I disagree. Recently, a person I know told me they now teach at the local community college and though I know this isn't true, it feels like I have somehow failed by not making those connections that would enable me to go be a guest speaker. I have many good things to share about working as a field medic and have already spoken a great deal at fire departments throughout the area.

Today, though, there was an amazing article in *Fire Rescue* magazine (August 2017) by Assistant Fire Chief Matthew Tobia who advised people to not always take promotions but to focus instead on doing what you like to do in your life. I found this to be similar to what Jim Collins writes about in *Good to Great:* find the intersection of doing what you like to do and what you do best. What I like to do and do best is taking care of others. All of these years I have *chosen* to take care of people on the front lines in the field, regardless of the money or prestige. As Chief Tobia writes, "Professional success does not equal personal happiness…it is easier to succeed when you are doing something you love." Chief Tobia would agree, I think, that I have the best of both worlds without the titles or rank. I get to take care of those in need as a medic (my external customers) and when I work on EMS supplies for Marion County, I make the firefighters' job of restocking far easier. I am helping those who help those in need (my internal customers). Regardless of pay or rank or others bossing me around sometimes like I am a novice, between these two tasks, I don't want to be anywhere else. I am thankful to be with Marion County Fire District #1 doing what I do best by helping those who call 911 and making my colleagues' job easier by keeping the EMS room supplied. Thank you Lord for helping me understand this about myself. As the Chief told me, "Leadership is often accomplished by example—not title."

Sometimes I think I must be important because I save lives and give comfort but then I remember that I am not important. In the Beatitudes, Jesus says, "Blessed are the humble in spirit, for theirs is the kingdom of heaven…Blessed are the humble, for they shall inherit the earth." (Matthew 5) God doesn't want us to be proud of our own merit but gives grace to the humble. Without the grace of God, I couldn't do what I have done for the last 37 years as a medic and before that as a chaplain and helper. "Give thanks to God. In everything give thanks to God." (1 Thessalonians 5:18)

I saw Don Fleck, a lifelong friend, at our Mt. Angel Fire Family Picnic and over the course of our conversation, I said I am destined to be the helper. He replied that being a helper was a pretty good place to be in life. Yes, when I was a Senior Minister Intern at Newport-Mesa Christian Church for Dr. George Wood, he called me the "Minister of Helps." My job *must* be to remain thankful for the opportunity to help others and to be just that, the "Minister Of Helps," the "Medic Of Helps," and the "Lawyer Of Helps."

Today I am working at the Oregon Convention Center after having come straight up here from Marion County Fire. There is an agriculture trade show along with an evangelical meeting in the building today. I ended up having a good chat with two people from the evangelical meeting.

My friend Bev Butler is an usher here today. I said hello to her when I was going into the trade show and as I walked by, she reminded me that I was her hero. I said, "What? No, I just do what I do." She then told me how I had taken good care of her with compassion and understanding at the Rose Quarter on February 23, 2006 at 6 p.m. when she got hurt, while others stood by laughing at her for getting injured. I was astonished she remembered that I was the one who took care of her and that I did my job with care and compassion. "You are my hero," she said to me. Maybe there is a reason I do what I do and that I get to do what I do best, by the grace of God.

> *Therefore, let those also who suffer according to the will of God entrust their souls to a faithful Creator in doing what is right.*
>
> *1 Peter 4:19*

AUGUST 26, 2017
Saturday

MATT AND I ARE AT THE Salem-Keizer Volcanoes baseball game tonight as a part of the Hometown Heroes night. A number of people are being recognized for their work in the community and Matt and I are being recognized for the code save we had earlier this year. The

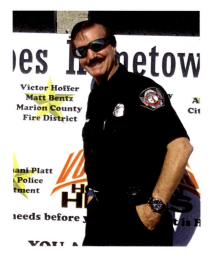

Me with the 2017 Volcanoes Hometown Heroes Banner featuring myself and Matt Bentz

man who we were able to revive after he died is now home alive and well and leading a normal life.

AUGUST 29, 2017
Tuesday

THESE LAST TWO DAYS HAVE BEEN incredibly busy. By the time we got the temporary medic checked off, we had to go to drill and then started getting a steady stream of calls right after we finished. We then picked up our regular ambulance from the repair shop, checked it off, and by the time we headed back to the station, it was 2:00 in the afternoon.

This is still the best place to be for me. I really am happy and thankful to be at Marion County Fire District #1. Yes, I do get frustrated over so many things that occur and how I am sometimes talked down to like a new medic. Just last week, I was reminded I am subordinate to everyone else, even the new hires coming on in September because I am a Medic only, not a firefighter. Such as it is in some people's eyes and that cannot be helped but I will continue to be a helper.

I was at the Oregon State Fair on Sunday and of course I had to buy ice cream from the Oregon Dairy Women's booth. This is a tradition going back to the years when I ran the medical team at the fair. Every night for eleven days straight I would eat ice cream from that booth. A while later, I was walking by Chef Rick's booth and he called out my name over the speaker system! I stopped to say hi and we had a pleasant conversation. I felt happy he still remembers me and by doing so, he reminded me I do make a difference in some small way. He is the best salesman I have ever heard and the kindest person.

ON SUNDAY MORNING IN MT. ANGEL, we responded to several difficult medical calls. One was for a stroke, another a fall, and one was a cardiac arrest. Sometimes no matter what we do, it's just not enough. On Saturday night we celebrated a code save and on Sunday, we couldn't prevent a death by bringing someone back to life. Strangely, this takes a greater toll on me now than it ever has during my 37 years of being a medic and I'm not sure why. Maybe I want to defeat death more than ever but sometimes death wins. I suppose Jesus is the only paramedic who can ultimately and permanently defeat death for us all.

> *For God so loved the world, that He gave His only Son, that whoever believes in Him should not perish but have eternal life.*
> *John 3:16*

John 3:16, which I consider to be the Gospel in a nutshell, provides us with the most important thing we can have in our lives: *simple faith.* God's love for us is fulfilled by our simple faith in Him. Today, go and show God's love for his children by helping those in need. Give to the poor, the widows, and the orphans, and quietly seek out those who need help without making it public.

Today has been a low-key day. After completely restocking the EMS room for the next few days, I ordered more supplies and completed the accounting paperwork. I also caught up on my charts, sent them to the hospital, mopped the floor, put away the dishes, and emptied the garbage.

Here at County, some people like to give me a hard time about being an old paramedic. That may be true, but I work hard at what I do. Often when they tease me, I tell them the story of the time I was walking down a path talking with God one sunny day. In the midst of the conversation, God stopped me, pointed at the side of the path, and asked, "Vic, what should we call that stuff?" I looked at it and answered, "What stuff, that dusty brown stuff, the terra firma?" "Yes, what should I call that?" "Well," I shrugged my shoulders, "how about 'dirt?'" See? If I named dirt, I must be older than dirt (as the firefighters and Captains like to remind me).

September

September 3, 2017
Sunday

WHAT A GREAT SHIFT TODAY! WE have already checked in all the supply orders, stocked the shelves, and went to a breakfast meeting where we enjoyed robust discussion about the incident command system and accountability. In this case, accountability is the keeping track of all the people on a scene of an incident. Right now, we use name tags called passports but we're always looking for ways to improve our system.

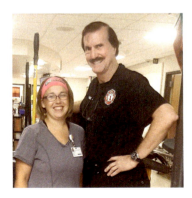

After breakfast, we ran several calls and on one of our runs to the hospital, I had an interesting talk with Lane, who is the Patient Flow Coordinator (PFC), and Kyleah.

Kyleah is the hardest working environmental services person in the emergency department. She cleans up every room and then takes care of the medic area for us. She is terrific and they are both kind people.

This evening I met with one of the firefighters for whom I had prepared a will. It was a pleasure to help him take care of this needed paperwork and he was happy to now have peace of mind about what would happen if he died. I knew that he, being incredibly athletic, spends a lot of time in the great outdoors along with the nurses and doctors from the hospital but he especially blessed my heart when he told me how I'm well respected by the hospital staff for the quality of my work and how I'm always courteous to the staff there. For my part, I am very fond of the people there and recognize how hard they work for the enormous amount of patients coming through their emergency department. I am glad to be where I am in my life—taking care of people and helping them feel better. At 4:30 this morning, we had a Mt. Angel Fire call for a sick patient before I was able to get ready to come over to Marion County Fire but I was able to still get here by 6:30 a.m.

Over the last twelve months of my probation, I've thought about my discouragements and things I still want to do and accomplish. It feels like my life's train schedule is different than the one God has for me. While my train is like a car flying down the tracks in Europe, God's train is the locomotive traveling up a hill at a far slower speed than I would prefer. I realize I'm still helping people and contributing to my community but it's on a different timetable than the one I wanted. I ask you to continue to believe and have faith alongside me. God is here for all of us and will always be there supporting us along the way. We just have different ideas of how fast we should get to our destination. Remember, "God is able to do exceeding abundantly beyond all that we ask or think, according to the power at work within us." (Ephesians 3:20) Believe the Lord will get you to where you want to go in life and where God knows you need to go.

It will also come to pass that before you call for help from God,
He will answer, and while you are still speaking and praying,
God will hear your prayer.

Isaiah 65:24

Let God hold you up.

Do you not know? Have you not heard?
The everlasting God, the Lord, the creator of the ends of the earth,
Does not become weary or tired,
His understanding is inscrutable.
He gives strength to the weary,
And to him who lacks might He increases power.
The children are exhausted and
The people all give up,
Yet those who have hope in the Lord
Will receive new strength;
They will fly like eagles,
They will run and finish the race,
They will walk and not fall down.

Isaiah 40:28-31

Good night, rest well, believe

I believe I am exactly where I'm supposed to be as God's servant and that God gives us each roles to fulfill. "He gave some as apostles, and some as prophets, and some as evangelists, and some as pastors and teachers, for the equipping of the saints for the work of service, to the building up of the body of Christ." (Ephesians 4:11-12) This gives me hope that even with my discouragements, failures, and sadness, I am meant to serve my community as a paramedic and helper. I encourage you to go out and serve *your* community, to feed the poor, help the widows and orphans, open your hearts to all people, and receive them with the love of Christ. God will be there for you.

At the hospital, I told Lane I had felt devastated when Salem Hospital Emergency Department told me I didn't have a job with them because I was too well educated and experienced. I'd spent all that time and money going to Certified Nursing Assistant School after they told me I *would* have a job and then it was taken away. Yet, it was ultimately for the best because now I'm here at Marion County Fire full-time, St. Paul Fire part time, Mt Angel Fire as a volunteer, all in addition to my work at the Convention Center. It's been a slow train getting here but I am where I am supposed to be.

In the movie *Gomer Pyle, USMC,* Gomer lost his voice and couldn't sing. He, too, felt devastated but the National Park Ranger told him he figured a hero was "a man doing the job he has to do, the best he knows how." I am no hero, but I am a person doing the job I have to do the best I know how. May God bless us all and keep us safe. Please pray for the firefighters, paramedics, and EMTs. We are all doing the job the best we know how.

SEPTEMBER 4, 2017
Monday – Labor Day

IT'S BEEN A FAIRLY GOOD DAY. We've only been moderately busy and managed to take a few breaks in between calls. At lunch, I choked on some of my food so I stopped eating. One of these days, I need to have a doctor check me out and give me an endoscopy to find out what's going on.

I recently found a statue of St. Francis of Assisi and heard of St. Francis again when watching an old episode of *Perry Mason.* I find that when I come across multiple references to something, I need to pay attention to what God is trying to tell me. St. Francis, for example, went through great difficulties growing up but overcame them and did many good works for the people and animals around him. Though St. Francis of Assisi did not write the Peace Prayer, it is often attributed to him and it holds great meaning for me.

PEACE PRAYER OF SAINT FRANCIS

Lord, make me an instrument of your peace:
where there is hatred, let me sow love;
where there is injury, pardon;
where there is doubt, faith;
where there is despair, hope;
where there is darkness, light;
where there is sadness, joy.
O divine Master, grant that I may not so much seek
to be consoled as to console,
to be understood as to understand,
to be loved as to love.
For it is in giving that we receive,
it is in pardoning that we are pardoned,
and it is in dying that we are born to eternal life.
Amen.

In all, it's been a great tour of duty. The evening has been fairly busy and in between calls, we managed to deliver new oxygen saturation cables for the EKG monitors to all the medics and engines. It's almost 11:00 p.m. now and I'm going to find something to eat for dinner before we go out on another call. Good night and may God bless us all.

SEPTEMBER 11, 2017
Monday

WOW! I'M SO EXCITED! I'M NOW off probation!

Victor Hoffer has successfully completed his one year of probation at Marion County Fire District #1!

This year and the few years before it have constantly challenged me as a person and, especially, as a person of faith. I have wanted the train to go fast and get me to my destination right away. Yet, I am here for now and it seems I will always be riding the slower train, quietly moving forward to my next test of patience and my next challenge of courage but enjoying the view the slower train affords.

I am so thankful to the many people who have believed in me and helped me throughout my entire life and, especially, throughout this last year. *Thank you.*

A Final Word

Thank you for taking this journey with me. Though it can be difficult to truly share our hearts, I believe it's vitally important for people to connect with each other's genuine human spirits—to know each other's joys, struggles, strengths, and weaknesses, and to be moved by them. It's in this spirit I have written my story as openly and honestly as I can and I thank you for honoring me with the time you have taken to read it.

The last two years have been difficult and frustrating for me. When I thought I would be hired here or there and it didn't happen, my hopes were dashed. Fortunately, the train stopped at Marion County Fire and I am extraordinarily thankful to be here and do not have a desire to go anywhere else. Even with my struggles, this is the best place for me to be serving the community. When coupled with Mt. Angel Fire, I believe I'm at the two best places to take care of people and to make a difference in other people's lives. My colleagues at Marion County Fire and Local 2557 have provided leadership and support for me and that support is deeply appreciated.

My many friends at the Salem Hospital Emergency Department have also stood strong with me throughout my struggles as I searched for the right path to walk. A few are pictured here and most are camera shy, so I just want everyone to know how great the nurses and doctors are and how the entire staff have supported me and believed in me and in my skills, knowledge and ability. If I begin to name them, I most certainly will leave some names out so suffice it to say, they are the hardest working group of people anywhere. They work so diligently taking care of the enormous and steady stream of people who come to their emergency department every day. They are the best people in the world.

Finally, I want us all to serve our communities. How you choose to do that will be up to you but beyond the specifics, there are three things we can all do. First, show respect and courtesy for all people. No matter who they are or what they believe or how they identify themselves, show respect, courtesy, and be a light of God's love for all humankind. Second, have faith and hope for your life and know you have a purpose in this world. Third, give to the poor, the widows, and the orphans with love and charity. Do all these things quietly, do them daily, and do them forever and always.

Show respect and courtesy.

Have faith and hope.

Give to the poor in love and with charity.

Victor Hoffer

PAUL AND VICTOR 3

*Paul played ball for the Oregon School for the Deaf (football),
John F. Kennedy High School (baseball), and Willamette Valley
Christian School (basketball). Three schools, three sports, and three all
league awards.*

Arizona
Go Wildcats!
"Bear Down"

FIRE CHIEF VIC HOFFER AND VICTOR 3

Be kind to one another,
caring and compassionate,
forgiving each other,
just as God in Christ also has forgiven you.

Ephesians 4:32

Acknowledgments

I don't know where to begin. My family, Lynell, Victor 3, and Paul have always believed in me and supported all my endeavors. My teachers, professors, and pastor have taught me so much about life and provided great examples of hard work and compassion as I have travelled this road of life. Thank you to my colleagues and friends who trust my judgment and medicine.

I appreciate my colleagues and friends at Marion County Fire District #1, Mt. Angel Fire District #15, St. Paul Fire District and Salem Fire Department, particularly Marion County Fire IAFF Local 2557 and Salem Fire IAFF Local 314. I would like to recognize the staff at Salem Hospital Emergency Department who are great, fantastic, and awesome hard working people who have supported me in my journey since 1980.

Thank you to my editor, Sarah Katreen Hoggatt, who helped me to polish and put most of what I have written into plain English. Finally, thank you to the Oregon State Fair Author's Corner for your encouragement to actually write.

Thank you all so very much for believing in me, supporting me, and helping me through my probie year and my entire life. Thank you.

Special dedication to those both living and those who have passed who have had great influence in my life:

My Parents and Family
Fire Chief Vic Hoffer and Mayor Margaret Hoffer
Lynell Hoffer, Victor Hoffer 3, and Paul Hoffer
Bob and Nella Hoffer, my godparents

Pastor
Reverend Dr. George O. Wood

Vanguard University
Reverend Dr. O. Cope Budge
Reverend Dr. Russell P. Spittler
Rosemary Jackson

Memorial Hermann Hospital
Dr. James "Red" Duke, M.D.
Reverend Dr. Julian Byrd
Reverend James Fawcett

Lewis & Clark Law School
Ronald Lansing
Susan Mandiberg
Henry Drummonds
Douglas Newell

Mt. Angel
Francis Piatz
Patricia and John Buchheit
Fire Chief Francis Schmidt
Larry and Shelly Andres
Joe Schmidt

Special Thanks
Marion County Fire District #1
Salem Hospital Emergency Department
and
my friends and colleagues

ABOUT THE AUTHOR

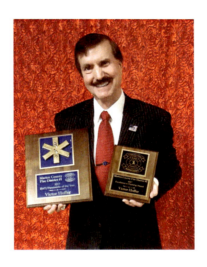

Victor Hoffer received the Paramedic of the Year Award for 2017 from Marion County Fire District #1. He also received the Excellence in Training Award for 2017. Victor remains a career paramedic with Marion County Fire.

In addition, he received the Paramedic of the Year Award for 2017 from Mount Angel Fire District #15. Victor continues to be a volunteer with Mt. Angel Fire, living out his legacy of community service started by his parents in Mt. Angel. His father was a firefighter-EMT for 41 years and the Fire Chief for 15 years and his mother was the Mayor of Mt. Angel.

Victor continues to practice law in Mt. Angel. His focus is on elder law, business law, and serving the disenfranchised and underserved in his community.

Victor also serves on the Oregon Transportation Safety Committee. The OTSC is the lead highway safety committee in Oregon. He was appointed to the committee in 2008 by Governor

Ted Kulongoski and Chair of the Committee by Governor Kate Brown in 2016.

EDUCATION, AWARDS AND HONORS

Victor Hoffer received the National Star of Life Award from the American Ambulance Association three times (1997, 2002, 2005). He was also recognized by Governor Ted Kulongoski with the Governor's Outstanding Lifetime Volunteer Achievement Award in 2010 and by the Oregon Health Authority with the EMS Cross (2004), a Community Service Medal (2007), and a Meritorious Service Medal (2012) for his service to EMS and the community.

Furthermore, Victor has received three Unit Citations from the OHA, one while with Woodburn Ambulance and two while with Metro West Ambulance.

He received the Paramedic of the Year Award from Washington County EMS in 1994 and two Excellence in EMS Awards in 1993 and 2000.

Victor Hoffer has a Juris Doctor from Lewis & Clark Law School, where he was Vice-President of the Student Council. He was accorded the highest honor at the law school, being selected as a member of the Cornelius Honor Society. He was the Phi Delta Phi graduate of the year, and received the Silver Key Award from the American Bar Association Law Student Division.

He received a Master of Arts degree from the Assemblies of God Theological Seminary, was a Divinity student at Fuller Theological Seminary, served as a student Chaplain at UCLA Medical Center, and completed a clinical internship in Pastoral Care at Memorial Hermann Hospital in conjunction with The Institute of Religion at the Texas Medical Center in Houston.

Victor received a Bachelor of Arts degree from Vanguard University of Southern California, formerly Southern California College in Costa Mesa. He attended Chemeketa Community College for his paramedic training.

He is steadfast in his commitment to serving all people and is happy and thankful to serve his community. As his sons have always confirmed, "You are doing what you are meant to do!"